BEST
BOOKS

FOR YOUR BIBLE STUDY
LIBRARY

CYRIL J. BARBER

This belongs to
Eva L. Lemons

LOIZEAUX
Neptune, New Jersey

BEST BOOKS
FOR YOUR BIBLE STUDY LIBRARY

© 2000 Copyright Cyril J. Barber

A Publication of Loizeaux Brothers, Inc.

*A Nonprofit organization Devoted to the Lord's Work and to the
Spread of His Truth*

Library of Congress Cataloging-in-Publication Data

Barber, Cyril J.
  Best books for your Bible study library / by Cyril J. Barber.
    p.cm.
  Includes bibliographical references.
  ISBN 0-87213-045-2 (pbk.: alk. paper)
  1. Bible—Study and teaching—Bibliography. I. Title.

Z7770.B37 2000
[BS600.2]
016.220'071—dc21   00-047802

Printed in the United States of America

10 9 8 7 6 5 4 3 2 1

ABOUT THE
AUTHOR
— ❧ —

C yril J. Barber has had a long career first as a librarian and educator and more recently as a pastoral counselor. Currently he is an associate pastor on the staff of Plymouth church in Whittier, California.

Dr. Barber holds degrees from American, British, and canadian institutions including Rosary College Graduate School of Library and Information Science (M.L.S., *cum laude*), Dallas Theological Seminary (M. Th.), and Biola University's Talbot Theological Seminary (D.Min., *magna cum laude*) and has been awarded two *honoris causa* D. Litt. degrees. He has served on the faculties of Trinity Evangelical Divinity School and Rosemead Graduate School of Psychology. At the Simon Greenleaf University School of Law he was the professor of bibliography, the dean of the Learning Resource Center, and a member of the Academic Senate.

Dr. Barber has authored numerous journal articles and more than thirty books including *Dynamic Personal Bible Study, Nehemiah and the Dynamics of Effective Leadership, Ruth: A Story of God's Grace, Judges: A Narrative of God's Power,* and a two-volume work on *The Books of Samuel*—all published by Loizeaux Brothers.

CONTENTS

1. JUST BETWEEN US   7

2. CHART AND COMPASS   17

3. WITHIN ARM'S REACH   25

4. THE WISDOM OF THE AGES   33

5. OUR LEGACY   53

BIBLIOGRAPHY   69

ACQUISITION CHECKLIST   82

CHAPTER 1

JUST BETWEEN US

— 🕮 —

No man is uneducated who knows the Bible,
and no one is wise who is ignorant of its teachings.
SAMUEL CHADWICK

How It All Began

In the first few hours after receiving Christ as my Savior, I realized that I would have to take personal responsibility for my spiritual growth. I could not leave my spiritual nurture to the church of which I was a member. The denomination to which I belonged at the time had a long and enviable history. Among its luminaries were devout individuals such as Handley C. G. Moule, Charles Simeon, and W. H. Griffith Thomas. Its missionaries were to be found on every continent and had evangelized many of the remote parts of the world. And included within the ranks of its theologians were such greats as H. P. Liddon, J. B. Lightfoot, B. F. Westcott, and scores of others whose names were at one time household words.

Why then did I feel it necessary to take responsibility for my own spiritual growth? The church body to which I belonged had fallen on hard times. Only a few of those graduating from the divinity schools of the approved universities were evangelical. Among these devout and godly individuals were Leon L. Morris, James I. Packer, and John R. W. Stott. But, as everyone knows, they are the exception and not the rule.

7

If I Can Do It

Nothing ever happens by chance, and both before I became a Christian as well as afterwards, I was conscious of the fact that the events of my life were under God's direct control. I was eighteen at the time of my conversion. Six years earlier, my parents had divorced, and I had been sent to a boarding school. To me, this was the ultimate form of rejection.

Then, at age fifteen, my education had been abruptly terminated. My grades were low and my father saw no need to pay for my schooling if I did not want to learn. So he wrote the principal telling him of his decision. I was shown the letter. I knew that at the end of that school year I would have to find a job and work to support myself.

Life was hard. Rent was high and I earned minimum wage. I was without skills and was forced to take night classes to finish high school. Then I took further studies at night to try and prepare myself for a career. With all of these demands, how was I to take care of my spiritual growth? It wasn't easy.

To compound the situation, six months after receiving the Lord Jesus as my Savior I was told to leave by the rector of the church I attended. No, I had not embraced some strange doctrine. I had become an unwitting irritant to him. He was angered over the fact that my conversion had taken place outside of the activities of "the church" and "his parish ministry." And so I left. But where should I go? I felt the pain of rejection all over again, coupled with feelings of loneliness and vulnerability.

The Lord, however, took care of me and led me to a Christian fellowship where I was accepted and loved. From that time onwards I identified with groups of believers that could best be described as independent and Bible-believing.

Building on a Solid Foundation

While talking with some Christian friends I was introduced to the writings of the late Henry A. Ironside. I read first one of his books then another. Most of his expositions were ordered at the rate of one a month through a bookstore I frequented. In time I read everything Dr. Ironside had written. You might say that I cut my spiritual teeth on his books. And I have never regretted the foundation that he laid for the development of my spiritual life.

I also developed friendships with older, more mature men and women, and I pestered them for recommendations of good books to read. The devotional writings of J. Wilbur Chapman, John Fletcher (of Madeley), F. B. Meyer, G. Campbell Morgan, H. C. G. Moule, Andrew Murray, Ruth Paxson, and C. H. Spurgeon were quickly added to the list of my favorite authors. The writings of these gifted individuals fed my spirit and increased my desire for more Bible study.

Of course, it wasn't long before some people started telling me about different schools of thought. They were generally down on dispensationalists, but no one could tell me why. All I got in answer to my questions was a potpourri of verbal vagaries. Now, as I look back on those years, I realize that my study of God's Word (using the best commentaries available) made these theological concerns of secondary importance.

In time I found that evangelicals were also divided over Calvinism and Arminianism. This discovery took place in the early 1950s, and I was shocked to learn that the feud had been going on for centuries. What was I to do? I listened to what was being said and on occasion found myself drawn into some heated arguments. These left me feeling miserable. I found that the best course of action was to return to a study of God's Word, aided by those writers whose works had been a blessing to me in the past. In time, issues came into focus in my mind and I can now look back with gratitude for the process through which I passed. Much later I realized that what I had done wasn't new. The apostle Paul had recommended it in one of the first letters ever written to a New Testament church. He had said, "Test everything. Hold on to the good" (1 Thessalonians 5:21).

As I expanded my reading, new names were added to my list of favorite authors. These included A. C. Gaebelein, A. T. Pierson, Charles C. Ryrie, W. Graham Scroggie, Lehman Strauss, Ray Stedman, and Warren Wiersbe.

For Your Encouragement

But someone will say, "Surely you have to be a bookworm, and reading all the time, to grow in your understanding of the Bible and the practice of your faith?" The answer is, "No, you don't." During the early years of my Christian walk I became active in the young people's fellowship of the church. I attended, taught Sunday school class, and served as a lay preacher. These activities were made possible because of what I had learned through my study of the Word. I owed whatever growth I made as a Christian to the variety and reliability of the books I read.

With half-an-hour's reading every night
as a steady practice, the busiest man
can get a fair education.
Sir William Osler, M.D.

Now it's time for a confession. And if my confession will be of encouragement to you, then please read on. I have failed every speed reading course I have ever taken. I still admire my friends who can read heavy treatises at a rate of eight hundred or more words per minute. My speed is a little over two hundred words per minute. I wish I could read faster, but in spite of all my efforts I have not been able to increase my speed. So if you are a tortoise like me, keep at it. There's more to life than racing like a hare to the finish line. We can truly savor a book. We can delight in apt descriptions or the turn of a particular phrase, and above all we can truly relish what we are doing. Our more gifted friends get winded just turning the pages.

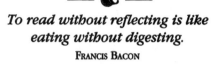

*To read without reflecting is like
eating without digesting.*

FRANCIS BACON

Some Guidelines

So as you take responsibility for your own spiritual growth here are a few guidelines:

- Choose your authors carefully. Obtain your recommendations wisely. Read judiciously.
- Read widely so as not to get into a rut. And be sure to include biographies. To these you should add church history, devotional works on prayer, et cetera, along with good expositions.
- Buy only those books that are worth keeping. Obtain what is of passing worth through inter-library loan either from your local public library or through your church library. Avoid ephemeral works. Often those on the "Top Ten" list this month will clutter the shelves of second-hand dealers a year from now.

In the course of time I left the shores of the United Kingdom for the United States. At that time I was able to take formal training in Biblical studies and library science. I thoroughly enjoyed these challenges! The titles I have included in this booklet are representative of the few books you could add to your home library. Many good ones have been omitted, since to include them all would have necessitated a larger volume. Use what is suggested here to get started.

Out-of-Print Titles

Some books that came highly recommended were out-of-print. At first I kept these titles in my head, but as the number increased, I began to write them down. After coming to the United States I found out that librarians call this a "wants list." I regularly sought for these hard-to-find books in the catalogs sent out by second-hand bookstores. Dr. Jerry Cramer issues a list of second-hand book dealers entitled *Cramer's Corner*. It covers Christian bookstores across the entire nation. His address is:

> Cramer's Corner
> c/o Boulevard Bible Church
> 5750 Louisiana Drive
> New Port Richey, FL 34654
> cramerscorner@cusave.com

There are scores of out-of-the-way shops. Your town or city, or a city close to you, has its haunts for book lovers, and I suggest that you consult the yellow pages of your local phone directory. Get to know the owners, and after they get to know you they will begin to look out for the kind of books they believe will be of interest to you.

Other reliable secondhand dealers who regularly send out listings of the books they have for sale are:

> Archives Bookshop
> 1396 East Washington Blvd.
> Pasadena, CA 91104
> archives@archivesbookshop.com

> Cornerstone Books
> P.O. Box 28224
> Santa Ana, CA 92799
> http://members.globalpac.com/CBOOKS

> Kregel Used Books
> P. O. Box 2607

Grand Rapids MI 49501-2607
usedbooks@kregel.com

Noah's Ark Book Attic
1500 Highway 246 North
Greenwood, SC 29649
noahsark@emeraldis.com

Arranging Your Books and Illustrations for Maximum Usefulness

As your personal collection of books begins to grow you will need to have a system to keep them in order. This is particularly important if you are a lay Christian worker or teach a home Bible study group or Sunday school class.

The Dewey Decimal Classification (DDC) system is the simplest and easiest to use. It is used in nearly all public libraries throughout the United States, and this would not be the case if it were not user-friendly. The DDC tables and area codes are contained in a four-volume set. It may be more conducive to your purpose to begin with *The Minister's Library* by C. J. Barber, available from the publisher of this booklet. Volume 1 begins with a very simple explanation of how you may wish to catalog and classify your library. Also included is a Subject Guide or Relative Index that gives the Dewey Decimal Classification for most of the subjects you will need.

A new book is still on trial , and an amateur is not in a position to judge it. It has to be tested against the great body of Christian thought down the ages. . . . It is a good rule, after reading a new book, never to allow yourself another new one till you have read an old one in between.

C. S. Lewis

Each volume of *The Minister's Library* also provides an annotated list of over 4,000 books that you may wish to be informed about. The complete classification data is to be found at the end of each entry. Volume 1 covers books published in the post-Reformation era, with specific concentration on the nineteenth and twentieth centuries. Volume 2 of *The Minister's Library* covers books published between 1971-1985. All entries in volumes 1 and 2, plus important titles published between 1986-1990, are now available in electronic format, and the database will be updated regularly.

One last matter before we draw this chapter to a close. As you become a productive Christian worker and/or Sunday school or home Bible class teacher you will want to keep your illustrations filed away so that you can find what you are looking for easily and with a minimum of wasted time. The system I use was devised by Dr. Haddon W. Robinson, the master homiletician of Gordon-Conwell Theological Seminary. I have been amazed at the ease with which this kind of filing system can be set up.

Basically it involves a set of 8.5" by 11" inch fifth-cut file folders—with one set of five folders for each letter of the alphabet. These are arranged so that the five raised sections form a row that stretches across the file drawer from left to right, with each file being assigned a *letter* of the alphabet and a *vowel*.

This is how it looks:

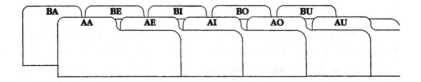

As you come across material you wish to keep, you ask yourself: "What subject or topic does this cover?" Let's say, for the sake of illustration, you have come across some material on *friendship* that you want to keep for possible future use.

The first letter is *f* and the first vowel is *i*, so you would place the information in the FI file. If the contents of an article or newspaper clipping deal with *abortion*, you naturally place it in the AO file. If it is on the *disciples* who followed the Lord Jesus during His earthly ministry, it would obviously go into the DI file. Information on *parenting* would go in the PA file.

In time a file might contain a variety of information—tearsheets from magazines or newspapers or data that you have collected or copied from different sources. For example, your AO file might contain material on topics like *abortion, adolescence, adoption, advocate* (Greek Word), *alcoholism,* and *astronomy.*

On those rare occasions when a word does not have a vowel (e.g. Egypt) use the *y* as an *i* and place it in the EI file. Very few items will necessitate such a subjective decision. In the final analysis this is the easiest and most efficient filing system that has been devised to date. And it is specifically developed by you with the descriptive terms you commonly use.

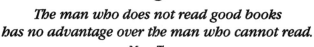

*The man who does not read good books
has no advantage over the man who cannot read.*

MARK TWAIN

CHAPTER 2

CHART AND COMPASS

— 🐌 —

The more profoundly we study this wonderful Book,
and the more closely we observe its precepts,
the better citizens we will become
and the higher will be the destiny of our nation.
WILLIAM MCKINLEY

It was a hot, humid day in Havana, Cuba. Even though it was the peak of the hurricane season, the convoy that lay at anchor in the harbor was anxious to get underway. But why the hurry? Simply put, the wealth of the New World was needed in Spain and the fleet commander had decided to risk any bad weather he and the twenty-eight ships under his command might encounter.

Among the vessels that tugged gently at their cables with each swell of the sea, there was the *Santa Margarita*. She was a proud 630-ton galleon that was now, in addition to her four-teen passengers, laden with a vast wealth of silver ingots, gold nuggets, silver coins, copper, and some perishable items like tobacco.

According to the ship's manifest and the records that were kept meticulously by the harbor master and agents of the king of Spain, these vessels began their journey back to the old World on Sunday, September 4, 1622. All went well for a time and the ships made good progress. Then, a day out to sea (Monday), a gale sprang that buffeted the tiny fleet. At first the ships kept their sailing positions, but when the wind rose to

17

hurricane strength the vessels lost sight of each other. Being powered by sail, little could prevent them from being dashed to pieces on the reefs and shoals of the Florida Keys. By sunrise on Tuesday the *Santa Margarita* was the only one left afloat.

Any thought of being spared the fate of the other vessels quickly vanished when a sudden shudder accompanied by the sound of splintering of wood indicated that it too had run aground on a reef . After that it was just a matter of time before huge waves broke open the hull. Most of the passengers were able to cling to pieces of wreckage and were picked up by passing ships after the storm subsided. But the treasures the ship was carrying were lost. These would be kept safe at the bottom of the ocean for centuries, covered by the shifting sands.

And so the years passed. Finally, after many people had tried to locate the *Santa Margarita* (by reading eye-witness reports, and carefully studying nautical charts and the records of other salvage operations that repose in the Archive of the West Indies), a man named Melvin Fisher began a search for the remains of the wrecked galleon. Using the latest scientific equipment (including a magnetometer), he and his colleagues were able to locate a wreck where broken Spanish pottery and a clump of encrusted silver coins marked the spot where a ship had gone down. But was this the *Santa Margarita*?

They continued their search and discovered three large gold bars. The search was now intensified. Several weeks later, more broken pottery, hundreds of silver coins, a nine-pound silver bell, silver plates, a sword, and a mariner's astrolabe were brought to the surface. But still there was no indication of the ship from which these treasures were taken.

After that, few artifacts were found. Each succeeding day brought little if anything of worth. Everyone knew that untold wealth lay on the sea floor, but where? The search had become a frustrating experience of trial and error. And if what they had found came from the *Santa Margarita*, then where was the rest of it?

It was then that Melvin Fisher's son joined the searchers. He donned his scuba gear and disappeared over the side of one of the search vessels. His personal, on-site inspection revealed two rows of silver ingots equidistant from each other, and a portion of a large wooden hull that had been remarkably well preserved.

Other divers joined him and they soon located a gold bar, two more large silver ingots, a 105-pound mass of silver coins (all stuck together), and a variety of other collectibles. What was most important, however, was five numbered silver ingots. When compared with the manifests of the *Santa Margarita*, these numbers matched. The ingots had been brought on board prior to her departure. Of course, the rest of the story is history.

THE JOY OF DISCOVERY

In Bible study, we follow the same principles Melvin Fisher used in his quest for sunken treasure.

- We diligently read the documents that have come down to us, looking for clues as to the theme and purpose of the Biblical writer. This process may involve both primary and secondary source materials.
- We consult maps and charts that will help us pinpoint with accuracy exactly where the events described in the "documents" took place.
- We familiarize ourselves with the precise meaning of words in the "manifest" (i.e., book of the Bible we are studying).
- We read what others have done as they engaged in a similar quest.

This chapter will focus your attention on those resources that you can use to make your study of God's Word an exciting experience.

— 🐚 —

The foundation of one's library should be good reference books, and how to use them should be learnt. One must have a concordance . . . and a good Bible dictionary . . . and then, of course, there must be good commentaries . . . .

W. GRAHAM SCROGGIE

— 🐚 —

Bible Atlases

One of your first needs will be a good Bible atlas. Almost every major publishing house in the United States has its own. The task of choosing a suitable one is awesome. Your quest will be shortened by consulting Dr. Barry J. Beitzel's *The Moody Atlas of Bible Lands*. It contains beautiful colored maps and pictures of the places described in the text, together with clear topographical diagrams and factual information that will enhance your knowledge of both the Old and New Testaments.

Some atlases, however, have not been written from a conservative theological point-of-view. One such work was produced by two Jewish scholars, Dr. Yohanan Aharoni and Dr. Michael Avi-Yonah. It carries the title *The Macmillan Bible Atlas* (3d edition, edited by A. F. Rainey and Z. Safrai). This atlas contains a wealth of information, but its dating of certain Old Testament events is not reliable. I began using this atlas when the first edition was published. This was long before Barry Beitzel's work appeared in print. Having grown used to it, I have continued to refer to it. In spite of its weakness in dating events, you may want to keep *The Macmillan Bible Atlas* in mind for a future investment.

Before we move on we need to say something about Dr. Carl Rasmussen's excellent *Zondervan NIV Atlas of the Bible*. It is included here because of its title. It is called an atlas, but in reality it is a beautifully illustrated historical geography of all peoples and places mentioned in the Bible. Of course, some maps have been interspersed throughout the text, but these are incidental to the purpose of the book. There are also diagrams, hand-drawn topographical charts, and everything to delight the reader.

Bible Dictionaries

Next, it is important for you to have a good, reliable Bible dictionary. A Bible dictionary is really a series of articles on Bible topics that have been arranged in alphabetic order (e.g., generally ranging from "Aaron" to "Zu'zim") and include archaeological, biographical, historical, social, cultural, and philological data.

Finding a good Bible dictionary is a little more difficult than you might at first imagine. Once again there seems to be almost as many Bible dictionaries as there are publishers. And not all of them are worthy of your time or attention. A good rule of thumb is, *don't buy an abridged Bible dictionary*. The material has invariably been truncated to accommodate the money allocated by the publisher with little or no thought being given to the needs of the user.

One of the handiest one-volume dictionaries is Merrill F. Unger's *New Unger's Bible Dictionary*, edited by Harrison, Vos, and Barber. It contains valuable current material on every book of the Bible, including information on the customs and culture of the peoples of the ancient Near East and the Mediterranean world, and is replete with archaeological information on the Dead Sea Scrolls and the major cities of the Old and New Testaments. Longer articles contain bibliographies that lead to other sources of information. All things considered, this is the best one-volume Bible dictionary for general use.

You will need only one good one-volume Bible dictionary. Should a need be felt for more information, then a multi-volume work like *The Zondervan Pictorial Encyclopedia of the Bible* (5 volumes) should be consulted. This work, while basically evangelical and containing articles by respected specialists, is not consistent. For example, data on Moses, the Exodus, and the history of the Old Testament will contain contradictory information. However, it is the best modern multi-volume dictionary/encyclopedia available at this time.

Bibles, Versions, and Concordances

There are numerous translations of the Bible, each with its own claim to fame. The most accurate version is the *New American Standard Bible* (NASB). It is available from a variety of dealers. The *New American Standard Exhaustive Concordance of the Bible* is an invaluable aid and comes complete with Hebrew, Aramaic, and Greek indices.

Another good translation is the *New King James Version* (NKJV), and is accompanied by *The NKJV Exhaustive Concordance*.

The most popular translation of the Bible is the *New International Version* (NIV). It is easy to read, but less accurate than the NASB and NKJV. The concordance that accompanies this version is *The NIV Complete Concordance*, edited by E. W. Goodrich and John R. Kohlenberger, III.

A Study Bible is often very helpful and Charles C. Ryrie has prepared *The Ryrie Study Bible* for the NASB, NKJV, and NIV. Each book of the Bible is introduced with a brief account of when it was written, and by and for whom. This is followed by a concise outline and notes on text.

Interlinear Testaments

Melvin Fisher's earthy quest for a lost fortune compelled him to become literate in Spanish (and possibly Portuguese and Latin as well) so that he could read manifests, letters, and other documents and memorabilia found in monasteries, vaults, and the archives of different cities throughout Central America, Spain, and Portugal.

We can use an interlinear translation to help us with the languages we may not have studied. Interlinear translations have a long history. They were first used in monasteries and

universities in medieval times. And they have been in use ever
since. By using an interlinear translation your fears of not being able to use the original languages need no longer deter
you from meaningful Bible study.

The Interlinear Hebrew/Greek English Bible edited by Jay
Green is a valuable acquisition. Volumes 1 through 3 of this
interlinear Bible cover the Old Testament. Volume 4, covering
the New Testament, is not as helpful as one might expect. It
was added to the Old Testament for the sake of completeness.
The Old Testament volumes, available separately and used
independently, will enable you to use scholarly commentaries
with good success.

The most valuable counterpart for New Testament study is
The NASB Interlinear Greek-English New Testament, which is
accompanied by the literal translation of Dr. Alfred Marshall.
This work has stood the test of time and has become the standard interlinear for the study of the New Testament. Its use
will enable you to use a variety of exegetical works that otherwise might have been unintelligible to you.

Word Studies

Because the Bible was written in Hebrew, Aramaic, and
Greek, sooner or later you will feel the need for a special book
that will explain to you the nuances of different words and
how their meaning may have changed with the passing of
time. To meet this need there is Vine's Expository Dictionary of
Old and New Testaments Words by W. E. Vine, Merrill F. Unger,
and William White, Jr. This book is, in reality, two books in
one. It combines Nelson's Expository Dictionary of the Old Testament by Drs. Unger and White with Vine's An Expository
Dictionary of New Testament Words.

As is to be expected, the new Vine's Expository Dictionary
is divided into two parts: (1) Old Testament, and (2) New Testament. Words used in either Testament are arranged in alphabetic order according to the English word. Synonyms can be
traced by consulting the indexes of English words in both

sections. *Vine's Expository Dictionary* is ideal for lay use. No knowledge of Hebrew or Aramaic or Greek is needed. It places within your reach a wealth of material through which you will be able to expand the scope of your studies and gain fresh insights into the meaning of words.

Other Essential Books

Also of great value is *A General Introduction to the Bible* by Drs. Norman L. Geisler and William E. Nix. These authors tackle the tough questions concerning the Bible's inspiration, canonization, transmission, and translation. There is an abundance of essential data to be found between these covers.

Another important work is John Phillips' *Bible Explorer's Guide*. It is divided into two parts, (1) Interpretation or Hermeneutics, (2) Helps. In this book Dr. Phillips surveys the different approaches to understanding the Bible. His material is concise and relevant.

After learning about the Bible, how it came down to us, and how it should be interpreted, the next important step is to focus on the ways to study different portions of the Bible. It is here that the book by Howard G. Hendricks and William Hendricks, *Living by the Book*, is the best on the market. It will amply repay the time spent mastering its contents.

— 🐦 —

Life being short and the quiet hours of it few,
we ought to waste none of them reading valueless books.

JOHN RUSKIN

CHAPTER 3
WITHIN ARM'S REACH

— 🐚 —

A respectable acquaintance with the opinions of the giants
of the past, might have saved many an erratic thinker from
wild interpretations and outrageous inferences.

CHARLES H. SPURGEON

Have you ever been to a new part of the country and felt lost or turned around so that it was difficult for you to find your way about? My wife and I revisited Jackson Hole and the Yellowstone National Park, Wyoming. There we saw once again the majestic Teton mountain range that towers twelve thousand to thirteen thousand feet above sea level without any foothills. We also journeyed northward into Yellowstone and looked in amazement at the variety of geysers and water-falls that attract hundreds of thousands of visitors each year.

As we drove through the forested areas of Yellowstone we were compelled to take a detour due to some extensive repairs that were being made to the road. The maps that were freely available to visitors were a great help, but they did not contain the roads we were required to take when we took the detour. And we did not know that two days of heavy winds had blown down some of the signs that were essential if we were to find our way back to the main road.

I'm not sure how lost we were, but I do know that wending our way through stands of thick trees, following the contour of hills and skirting geysers, did cause us to lose our sense of

25

direction. It was only as some landmark appeared that we were able to find out where we were. And it is the identifiable landmarks of Scripture that keep us from becoming lost mentally (through man-made philosophy), emotionally (through false psychology), relationally, and spiritually.

BIBLE COMMENTARIES

Some people have the mistaken impression that if they have a single volume commentary on the whole Bible (or even a two-volume commentary) that is all they need. Such works are numerous, but teachers, lay preachers, and for the most part, Sunday school Christian workers find them too limited to be of any lasting value. So be warned, don't invest in superficial studies on the Bible.

There is a process through which a commentator should pass before he or she begins to write a commentary. This process begins with exegeis (i.e., a thorough knowledge of the original text) that unfolds the Biblical writer's theme or purpose. When this theme is properly understood the writer can then progress on to exposition and explain the text with all the skill at his or her command. Finally, the devotional use of the Bible should be consistent with the meaning of the words used by the original writer and the purpose of the Biblical writer. The process is: Exegesis > exposition > devotion.

The Bible is a lot like a map in that it serves as our guide through the highways and byways of life. Its diverse literature contains something for every contingency we may be called upon to face. However, as anyone who has faced trials and difficulties knows, it is easy to get turned around and become confused or lost when we are buffeted by the repeated vicissitudes of life.

But someone is sure to voice an objection to making the Bible the chart and compass of life. "Surely," they will say, "the Holy Spirit has been given to guide us. Why then do we need the Bible or books that explain the Bible?" To that honest question our answer is that while it is true the Holy Spirit indwells us, it is wrong for us to neglect what He has given us. He inspired the writers of the Old and New Testaments to write the books that have come down to us, and He uses this information to guide and embolden us for the trials we face. Bible study is not an end in itself. Its purpose is to make us mature in Christ (1 Corinthians 2:10-16; Hebrews 5:13–6:2) by bringing us into conformity to His image (2 Corinthians 3:18). To neglect its teaching is to cut ourselves off from the help we need. And if we allow this to happen we ultimately suffer irreparable loss. So let us never forget that to fellowship with the Lord in the light of His Word is to gradually become like Him.

Commentaries on the Whole Bible

Early on in my Christian experience I became aware of the writings of the late A. C. Gaebelein, and in particular his *Annotated Bible*. It was a multi-volume set and I pondered for weeks over whether or not to buy it. It has now been published unabridged in a single volume of 1,237 double-column pages under the title *Gaebelein's Concise Commentary on the Whole Bible*. It is worthy of your investment of time as well as money. Once you have purchased it, you can begin to read it slowly and reflectively. Dr. Gaebelein was a devout Christian. He followed a consistent, literal interpretation of Scripture, and he knew well those apparent detours that are often glossed over by less proficient guides.

Another work of merit is Dr. J. Sidlow Baxter's *Explore the Book*. Like Gaebelein's work it appeared first as a multi-volume set. It, too, has now been combined into a single large volume. Dr. Baxter's guide has many benefits. It is like a maverick. It is evangelical, but without bearing the brand of any particular denomination or group. And there is much value in Dr. Baxter's presentation. But his approach also has its limitations. Dr. Baxter uses the King James version of the Bible, and as a consequence did not benefit from the accurate nuances in newer translations that sometimes serve as shafts of light on some Bible doctrine or topic. These errors excepted, *Explore the Book* is still a helpful volume.

Another work that is worthy of close and repeated use is W. Graham Scroggie's *The Unfolding Drama of Redemption*, 3 volumes. It is exceedingly valuable for its overall emphasis, and lay preachers will find that it contains a wealth of usable material.

Commentaries on the Old Testament

Merrill F. Unger was one of the outstanding Old Testament scholars of our generation. His *Unger's Commentary of the Old Testament*, 2 volumes, treats each passage clearly and concisely while paying close attention to God's progressive revelation.

Commentaries on the New Testament

The New Testament counterpart to Merrill Unger's commentary is Warren W. Wiersbe's *Bible Exposition Commentary*, 2 volumes. For the past twenty years Dr. Wiersbe has been issuing small, readable commentaries on every book of the New Testament. Now these handy works have been combined into an attractive set. We are most grateful to Dr. Wiersbe for making these volumes available to us.

Another series on the entire New Testament is William Barclay's commentary on the New Testament (18 volumes including index) known as the *Daily Study Bible* series. While Dr. Barclay's theology often disappoints us, his illustrations from Greek literature have endeared him to people throughout the English-speaking world. In addition, his references to the history of the times or the manners and customs of the lands lying around the Mediterranean, are most apropos.

Of real worth is Charles R. Erdman's *Commentary on the New Testament* (17 volumes). The contents of each slender volume explain the argument of each New Testament book.

One's appreciation for Dr. Erdman grows the more his books are used.

I have already mentioned my indebtedness to the late Dr. Harry Ironside. He wrote a commentary on every book of the New Testament, and his treatments are of considerable value for their simplicity and warmth. He laid a foundation for my understanding of the New Testament that I continue to build on to this day (cf. 1 Corinthians 3:11-15).

BIBLE DOCTRINE

In his "Ballad of East and West," Rudyard Kipling wrote:

> Oh, East is East, and West is West,
>   and never the twain shall meet,
> Till Earth and Sky stand presently
>   at God's great Judgment Seat.

Of course England's great teller of tales was talking about Occidental and Oriental cultures, but if he were alive today he might be persuaded to write something similar about theologians and their systems of thought. Someone uninitiated in the different "schools" could easily look at the various theological positions and conclude that they are as far apart as east and west. And it might seem that at no time in history has division within the church been greater than at the present time.

Of the major schisms—Calvinism vs. Arminianism, conservative vs. liberal, and Calvinist/Reformed vs. dispensational—we will focus on the last. The others can be traced through the writings of those individuals mentioned at the end of this section.

To try and resolve the tension between Reformed theologians and dispensationalists, and to show what these systems have in common, Dr. Robert P. Lightner wrote his *Evangelical Theology: A Survey and Review*.

There is something most interesting about the author and

the publisher of this book. Dr. Lightner serves on the faculty of Dallas Seminary, and so it might be thought that he would produce a work out of a closed dispensational system of thought. And the publisher, Baker Book House, is a bastion for the promotion and promulgation of Reformed theology. What could ever bring these supposedly antagonistic ideologies together? Or, why would Dr. Lightner give his book to Baker Book House, and why would Baker Book House publish it?

The answer lies in the fact that the differences between these theological systems are very slight, and it is time these supposedly antithetical schools of thought emphasized the areas in which they are agreed rather than those in which they disagree. And this is what Dr. Lightner has done. His book demonstrates that there can be mutual understanding and respect between dispensationalists and Reformed theologians. We commend, therefore, Robert Lightner's *Evangelical Theology* to all who wish for a sound, evangelical statement of faith.

Another work of merit is P. Paul Enns' *Moody Handbook of Theology*. The uniqueness of his work is to be found in the simplicity of his style, and his synthesis of Biblical, historical, and theological material. Such an approach is necessary, for the church's doctrines were often developed in the furnace of controversy. Dr. Enns has succeeded in including historical data without unnecessarily encumbering the text.

Information about other worthy works by writers of the caliber of Louis Berkhof, John Calvin, Lewis Sperry Chafer, Charles G. Finney, Charles Hodge, John Miley, Charles C. Ryrie, and B. B. Warfield, et cetera, can be obtained by consulting the pages of *The Minister's Library*, I:232-283; II:167-229.

All denominations of Christians have really little difference in point of doctrine—embracing the virgin birth, sinless life, atoning death, bodily resurrection, and second coming of Christ—though they may differ widely in external forms.

SAMUEL JOHNSON

CHURCH HISTORY

The study of church history, for those who have never tackled the subject before, is much like plowing a field. The ground seems resistant to the blade of the plough. With perseverance, however, a framework can be established into which the controversies and doctrines of the centuries can be integrated. The best one-volume church history is Earle E. Cairns' *Christianity Through the Centuries*. Dr. Cairns is an evangelical and his handling of the different movements within Christendom is judicious without becoming tedious. In fact, by the time you finish his book you may find yourself wishing for another work to flesh out issues that are of importance to you. And if you do, you can again consult *The Minister's Library*, I:401-437; II:431-475. You can also look at the pages on apologetics (Christianity's defense of its beliefs), the growth of the creeds, the notable people who labored for Christ and His Kingdom, the rise of the *isms*, and much, much more.

In our next chapter we will look at specific works that will further open up to you the limitless wealth of God's Word.

There is nothing in life more wonderful than faith—the one
great moving force which we can neither weigh in the
balance nor test in the crucible.
SIR WILLIAM OSLER, M.D.

CHAPTER 4

THE WISDOM OF THE AGES

— 🐚 —

The family Bible is more often used to adorn coffee tables or
press flowers than it is to feed souls and discipline lives.
CHUCK COLSON

As a general rule, commentaries (whether in sets or on individual books of the Bible) fall into one of three primary groups: exegetical, expository, and devotional. Some exponents on the subject of Bible commentaries like to add two other kinds: homiletical and critical. And there is some validity to their advocacy of these divisions. The former is primarily for preachers, while the latter is for scholars. However, devotional and expository commentaries may follow a homiletic format, and exegetical commentaries are invariably critical.

Our purpose is not to introduce you to the heavy, technical works that require a mastery of the original languages (and at times French and German as well). We want to concentrate on devotional commentaries that will be a blessing to you and enrich your life. When necessary, we will include the occasional good exposition that may not have quite the same devotional content as some of the other volumes we suggest.

THE PENTATEUCH

We are familiar with the word *Pentagon*—the five-sided building where the "movers and shakers" of our nation's defense have their offices. Our word *Pentateuch* comes from the same root and is used to describe the first five books of the Bible that were written by Moses. A knowledge of them is essential to an understanding of the remainder of God's Word.

Here are two books that adequately treat the diverse themes of the Pentateuch. Dr. Victor P. Hamilton's *Handbook on the Pentateuch* is non-technical and enables the reader to grasp the overall theme of each book. And Dr. G. H. Livingstone has placed us all in his debt with *The Pentateuch in Its Cultural Environment.* He ably introduces his readers to the people of the ancient Near East and also writes about the habits and customs of the times. He is more technical than Hamilton, but well worth reading.

From these works we realize that the Lord wanted His people to be free and live joyful productive lives. And He gave them the rules that were to govern their lives, individually as well as corporately.

When we begin to study a book of the Bible it will be to our advantage if we select two or three commentaries that will introduce us to this portion of God's special revelation. Those who minister to us need to have access to a library of four thousand to five thousand hand-picked volumes. No such burden is laid on the layman. Two or perhaps three good books on each Biblical book will probably serve your needs adequately.

Genesis

Of the many commentaries on Genesis we will mention only three: John J. Davis's *Paradise to Prison*, John Phillips's *Exploring Genesis*, and W. H. Griffith Thomas's *Genesis: A Devotional Commentary*.

In *Paradise to Prison* Dr. Davis takes us on an excursion from the delights of the Garden of Eden that Adam and Eve enjoyed to the prison in Egypt where Joseph was incarcerated.

His treatment is excellent, and his handling of the historical and cultural features of Genesis is admirable.

Exploring Genesis is a well organized study guide that serious lay students of God's Word will welcome. Dr. Phillips' discussion of controversial issues is in the best evangelical tradition.

Genesis: A Devotional Commentary was first published in 1940, and I have gone through several copies, underlining each one and making notes in the margin. While Dr. Thomas is weak in his treatment of Genesis chapters 1–11, he is superb in his handling of chapters 12–50. Anyone wanting to teach on the lives of Abraham, Isaac, Jacob, and Joseph must read this book!

Exodus

An old work that still contains a wealth of valuable material is *Commentary on Exodus* by George Bush (2 volumes). It is dated archaeologically and historically, but Dr. Bush's devotional thoughts on the text more than make up for the deficiencies in those areas.

A modern commentary bringing out the theology of Moses' second book is R. Alan Cole's *Exodus: An Introduction and Commentary* in the Tyndale Old Testament Commentaries series. Dr. Cole shows an awareness of the issues and his overall handling of the text is to be commended.

Leviticus

Once again we are indebted to George Bush for his *Notes on Leviticus*. Not everyone can write with flare on Israel's sacrifices and offerings, rituals and standards of righteousness, but Dr. Bush has done so with skill that commands our admiration.

Roland K. Harrison, while more technical, never disappoints us. His *Leviticus, An Introduction and Commentary* in the

Tyndale Old Testament Commentaries series treats adequately the rites and regulations, sacrifices and offerings of God's ancient people, Israel.

And not to be overlooked is Lehman Strauss' *God's Prophetic Calendar*. Dr. Strauss concentrates on the feasts of Leviticus, chapter 24, and shows how each one prefigures some aspect of the work of salvation/redemption.

Numbers

Numbers is one of those books of the Old Testament that people find it easy to neglect. It begins with a genealogy and that is enough to put them off studying it. But Dr. Charles R. Erdman's *The Book of Numbers* is so helpful that he quickly overcomes one's initial skepticism. Furthermore, his explanation of the contents is vitally important to an understanding of Israel's history.

To complement Erdman's study there is Gordon J. Wenham's *Numbers: An Introduction and Commentary* (Tyndale Old Testament Commentaries series). Dr. Wenham's comments are brief, but he has a sense of what is important, and readily shares essential information with his readers.

Deuteronomy

There are many good discussions of Deuteronomy, but we will limit our recommendations to two: Charles R. Erdman's *The Book of Deuteronomy*, and Samuel J. Schultz' *Deuteronomy: The Gospel of Love* in the Everyman Bible Commentary series.

As always, Dr. Erdman gently eases his readers into the thought patterns and chief burdens of Israel's great law giver. His book is a good one to read if you have not studied the book of Deuteronomy before. Dr. Schultz' approach is different. He picks up on the fact that in this book Moses underscores the love of God for His people. This emphasis becomes the basis of his exposition.

There is no solid basis for civilization but in the Word of God. If we are to abide by the principles taught in the Bible, our country will go on prospering....The Bible is a book... which teaches man his own individual responsibility, his own dignity, and his equality with his fellowman.

DANIEL WEBSTER

THE HISTORICAL BOOKS

The civil and religious principles that God gave His servant Moses were designed to enable His people to lead righteous lives. This would result in their enjoyment of His blessings. By living in obedience to His commandments, judgments, and ordinances Israel would not only prosper, but also become a light to the nations. Their obedience was to be the key to blessing.

The messages of Deuteronomy were given while the people were camped on the eastern bank of the Jordan River waiting to enter the promised land. How they gained control of the main trade routes and cities is described for us in the book of Joshua.

Joshua

There are many delightful commentaries on the book of Joshua. Foremost, from a devotional point of view, is William G. Blaikie's *The Book of Joshua*. He treats in a most admirable manner Israel's conquest of the land, and his devotional thoughts are apropos to daily living.

Of a different nature is P. Paul Enns' *Joshua* in the Bible Study Commentary series. Dr. Enns is well-organized and treats each section briefly yet adequately. His handling of difficulties (e.g., the sun standing still in Joshua 10) is well done.

Judges

The book of Judges has been neglected for many years. Part of the problem may be traceable to early Bible teachers who emphasized the "failure motif" of the book (departing from the Lord, apostasy, discipline at the hands of an enemy, followed by repentance and restoration, only to begin the cycle all over again).

In *Judges: A Narrative of God's Power*, C. J. Barber takes a different approach. He stresses instead how the Spirit of God came upon an individual, empowering him or her for service. This same principle is then applied to believers today. Dr. Ray Stedman wrote of this work, "The parallels between the times of the judges and our modern difficulties and challenges are often uncanny....Anyone who reads the author's book will never forget the lessons of the judges and their pertinence to life today."

George Bush, in his *Notes of Judges*, does a masterful job of recreating the milieu of the era of the Judges, and his comments on the text will enhance one's understanding of and appreciation for this era of Biblical history.

Ruth

There are many worthy treatments of this pastoral idyll, and one of them is *Ruth: A Story of God's Grace* by C. J. Barber. In the Foreword to this book, Dr. Frederick A. Tatford wrote: "[The author] has deftly and capably demonstrated the relevance of Ruth's story to the present day. Not only has he given us an extremely satisfying exposition...but he has deduced from it many lessons. Here is a book that deserves to be read and then reread."

Arthur E. Cundall and Leon L. Morris were teamed to provide an exposition of *Judges and Ruth* in the Tyndale Old Testament Commentary series. Cundall on *Judges* is not as conservative as Morris on *Ruth*, and he makes numerous concessions to later redactors. Morris, however, is wise in his comments on the text and is to be commended for having given us an exposition that is true to the Scriptures.

The Books of Samuel

The life of David has attracted many writers and so there is no lack of good commentaries on these books. Joyce G. Baldwin has written *1 and 2 Samuel* in the Tyndale Old Testament Commentary series. While at times basing her exposition on the real or imagined symmetry of the text, and making allowance for different editors, her comments are generally relevant and helpful.

A fresh approach in a two-volume set is *The Books of Samuel*, by C. J. Barber. In the first volume, Dr. Warren Wiersbe wrote of it, "The book is a joy to read. . . . [The author] makes ancient history exciting and practical, and he does so without spiritualizing the text."

Also of great value are William G. Blaikie's *The First Book of Samuel* and *The Second Book of Samuel*. He expounds the text in a most capable manner and his devotional thoughts are always on target. Each volume is rich in historic detail and will amply repay the reader for time spent on them.

The Books of Kings

The works by Thomas Kirk and George Rawlinson have been combined into one volume under the title *Studies in the Books of Kings*. Kirk's comments on the life of Solomon fill a long-felt void, and Rawlinson's studies cover deftly and concisely the lives of the kings of Israel and Judah. All things considered, this is one of the most satisfying volumes extant.

Christopher Knapp follows the same general format as Rawlinson in his book *The Kings of Judah and Israel*. He traces the characteristics and accomplishments of each reign and correlates the lives of the kings with the ministry of the prophets whom the Lord sent to minister to His people.

First and Second Chronicles

There are few good expositions on these books. For the most part the Books of Chronicles have been neglected. Two books, however, will serve the purposes of the lay Bible student. They are John Sailhamer's *First and Second Chronicles* in the Everyman's Bible Commentary series, and Michael Wilcock's *The Message of Chronicles* in The Bible Speaks Today series.

Dr. Sailhamer recounts the history of the period with real insight into what is important, and Michael Wilcock has captured the essence of the Biblical writer's thought that he elaborates on as he expounds the theme.

Ezra, Nehemiah, and Esther

Walter F. Adeney has given us *Ezra and Nehemiah*. He brings to light a long-neglected period of Israelite history, and his discussion of Israel's fortunes and misfortunes is most helpful.

A work that focuses solely on the Book of Nehemiah is *Nehemiah and the Dynamics of Effective Leadership* by C. J. Barber. It has been described as "An unusual book that is both a commentary on Nehemiah and an excellent handbook on leadership....It is probably the most unique treatment of Nehemiah ever written" (Ministry in Focus).

— 𝕒 —

The Bible was never intended to be a book for scholars and specialists only. From the very beginning it was intended to be everybody's book, and that is what it continues to be.

F. F. BRUCE

— 𝕒 —

The late Harry A. Ironside provided us with *Notes on Ezra, Nehemiah, and Esther*. His style was very practical, and he possessed the unique ability to expound Scripture so that everyone could understand what a particular passage taught.

A good work on Esther is Alexander Raleigh's *The Book of Esther*. His study is refreshing in its approach and richly rewarding in its devotional comments on the text. It should not be neglected.

THE POETICAL BOOKS

With the book of Job we move from the section of the history of the Old Testament and into a section of the canon that contains the poetry of God's people. For fuller coverage of this section, see *The Minister's Library*, Volume I:144-152, and Volume II: 97-104.

Job

There are many expositions of the book of Job that focus attention on the nature and reason for suffering. Before one can properly understand the role of suffering in the plan and purpose of God, he or she should first master the contents of the book of Job unencumbered by special criteria.

Francis I. Anderson's *Job* (Tyndale Old Testament Commentary series) is helpful and easy to read. His critical theory of the composition of the book and the time when it was written leave much to be desired. However, his treatment of the text is generally of great value.

Roy B. Zuck's *Job* (Everyman's Bible Commentary series) condenses all of the comments on the text into 13 chapters. His material is well written and he not only explains the theme of the book, but also discusses the lessons to be learned from it.

Psalms

There are many good commentaries on the book of Psalms. One exposition that is worthy of serious consideration is J. J.

Stewart Perowne's *Commentary on the Psalms*, 2 volumes. Dr. Perowne highlights the diversity of content, and treats the unique features of Christ's (i.e., Messiah's) work. This is most helpful, for the question often arises, How can the psalmist, writing out of his own experience, prefigure Christ's agony or describe the things that happened to Him, or pertain to His future Kingdom? Dr. Perowne's answer is most satisfying.

Another work that always rewards the careful reader is John Phillips' *Exploring the Psalms*, 2 volumes. Each study is well outlined and the exposition of each segment is in the best evangelical tradition. Dr. Phillips is to be commended for his diligence in carrying this project through to its completion. This is one of the best works available today.

Proverbs

Proverbs has been referred to as "the laws of Heaven for life on earth." William Arnot's *Studies in Proverbs* is valuable for its insights and spiritual direction. He omits chapters 7 and 21 without explanation. However, for inspirational reading, this book is virtually without a peer.

Also of value is H. A. Ironside's *Proverbs* in which he expounds the text in a pleasing and refreshing manner. And not to be ignored is the work by George Lawson entitled *Commentary on Proverbs*. For all his erudition, Dr. Lawson's style is simple and practical. Those who possess a copy of this book will readily testify to its intrinsic worth.

Ecclesiastes

Ecclesiastes has been long neglected. Now, however, fresh interest has been aroused in its message. Walter C. Kaiser, Jr., in *Ecclesiastes: Total Life* (Everyman's Bible Commentary series), provides one of the finest introductions to the scope and meaning of Ecclesiastes that has ever been penned. In developing his theme, Dr. Kaiser points to the basic hunger in the heart of man for a meaningful and satisfying relationship with the Lord.

Derek Kidner does not believe that Solomon wrote Ecclesiastes. His book, *A Time to Mourn, a Time to Dance: Ecclesiastes and the Way of the World* (The Bible Speaks Today series), presents the theme as man's quest for God. He shows how all things result in disappointment and disillusionment, and that only a dynamic relationship with the Lord truly satisfies.

Of the many books written by Charles R. Swindoll, his best is his exposition of Ecclesiastes entitled *Living on the Ragged Edge*. In it he shows the relevancy of the court preacher's message to the present day. Swindoll's strength lies in his ability to relate passages from the Bible to everyday problems and dilemmas.

Song of Solomon

Solomon's Song has been subjected to a variety of interpretations. Basically these center in a two-character theory (Solomon and the Shulamite), and a three-character theory (Solomon, his bride, and her shepherd lover away in the hills); and whether the Song is an allegory of God's love for us or the delights of human love. The majority of Bible scholars today favor the two-character theory, and the trend of informed scholarship is toward a literal interpretation of the passage.

G. Lloyd Carr's *The Song of Solomon* (in the Tyndale Old Testament Commentary series) has gained a high degree of respectability since making its debut. His verse-by-verse comments are often quite helpful, and his insights into the dyadic relationship of husband-wife is designed to enlighten as well as challenge his readers.

S. Craig Glickman's *A Song for Lovers*, contains the author's own translation accompanied by pertinent comments on the text. He follows a literal interpretation of the subject matter, but moves the wedding to the beginning of the book instead of leaving it where Solomon inserted it. Glickman succeeds in prompting his readers to think about their own marriages.

H. A. Ironside's *The Song of Solomon*, favors the allegorical interpretation (i.e., the love of Christ for His church). His rationale for this approach remains one of the best.

When you marry, it's not because you've found the best [spouse] in the whole world, but because you've found one about whom you care very much, and you [decide] to share your life with that person, faults included.

PHYLLIS REYNOLDS NAYLOR

THE PROPHETIC BOOKS

This section of the Old Testament canon begins with Isaiah and ends with Malachi. It parallels Israel's history beginning during the divided monarchy and ending when prophetic revelation ceased. Several books have been devoted to the ministry of the prophets in Israel. They include Leon J. Wood's *The Prophets of Israel* and Edward J. Young's *My Servants the Prophets*. Each one is worthy of serious consideration.

Isaiah

Joseph A. Alexander wrote extensively on the book of Isaiah. His works included a commentary on the Hebrew text as well as a shorter study better suited to the needs of lay people. This latter work, *Isaiah, Translated and Explained* (2 volumes), is ideal for those desiring a simple exposition of the scope of Isaiah's prophecies.

William Kelly's *An Exposition of the Book of Isaiah* fills a long-standing need for a thorough treatment that faces squarely the difficulties of interpretation, and at the same time is able to interpret all that the prophet wrote about in light of the Messianic kingdom.

Jeremiah and Lamentations

Once again Charles R. Erdman has provided a good synopsis of the contents of these books with his readable *Jeremiah and Lamentations: An Exposition.* He also applies the text in practical ways.

Of great value is Charles L. Feinberg's *Jeremiah, a Commentary,* in which he makes the life and message of God's spokesman relevant to our time. Dr. Feinberg discusses the reasons for Judah's demise and shows how the Lord was working behind the scenes to accomplish His will. And not to be neglected in this very capable commentary is the reason for the rise and fall of the nations of the Near East. This work meets the need for a handy, gratifying exposition.

Then, Roland K. Harrison has given us *Jeremiah and Lamentations* (Tyndale Old Testament Commentaries series). He offers a brief, well-outlined and well-informed exposition.

And Walter C. Kaiser, Jr., has written *A Biblical Approach to Personal Suffering,* which is really a commentary on Lamentations. He discusses the causes of suffering and describes how the Lord ferrets out our sins so that we may confess our wrongdoing and He may be gracious to us. We also find in Dr. Kaiser's exposition a Biblical guide for managing grief, and this is of the utmost help. His book is to be highly recommended.

Ezekiel

Ezekiel was one of the people taken into exile by Nebuchadnezzar. His prophecy was written in the land of his captivity, Babylon.

Ralph Alexander's *Ezekiel* (Everyman Bible Commentary series), ably combines scholarship with a warm devotional style. His handling of the text is adequate, and he does not bore his readers with expansive discussions of theological trivia. His work is well balanced, and lay people will find it an ideal aid to use in their discussion groups.

P. Paul Enns presents a wealth of information in his *Ezekiel* (in the Bible Study Commentary series). He keeps before the reader what God's will is for His chosen people, the Jews, and where Gentiles enter the picture. And he is not afraid to offer his own opinion on specific issues. This is done in good taste, and readers will arise from a study of this book stronger in their faith and more assured of God's plan for all His people.

The renowned British Bible scholar, Frederick A. Tatford wrote *Dead Bones Live: An Exposition of the Prophecy of Ezekiel*. His work is masterful in every way. Dr. Tatford resisted the temptation to treat certain sections of the prophecy as allegories, and maintained instead a consistent literal interpretation. Readers will find some material within these covers that will surprise them (e.g., the reinstitution of animal sacrifices in the millennium). Dr. Tatford's discussion of this portion of Ezekiel is particularly appropriate.

Daniel

It would be very easy to recommend two dozen good books on Daniel. That is not the purpose of this slender volume, and so reference should be made to *The Minister's Library* (I:157-159; II:108-110) for the essential works on this prophet and his prophecy.

The writings of Robert Duncan Culver are always worth reading, and his book entitled *Daniel and the Latter Days* (which must not be confused with his *Histories and Prophecies of Daniel*) is a must! Dr. Culver is a fine theologian. He has worked through the issues and drawn his own conclusions. He presents the different schools of thought in clear, concise terms, and then offers his own ideas based on an extensive examination of the original text. Here is a work that can be read with confidence.

John Phillips and Jerry Vines, two accomplished expositors, have teamed up to give us *Exploring the Book of Daniel*. Their material is ably outlined and presented with clarity and conviction. This is an ideal work for those who have not studied the book of Daniel before.

Frederick A. Tatford's *Daniel and His Prophecy*, treats God's prophetic word with great respect. He does not probe minutiae, but instead explains the gist of each vision in such a way that the reader is able to see how the many strands of evidence dovetail together. Here is a work lay people will enjoy.

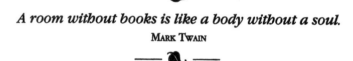

A room without books is like a body without a soul.

MARK TWAIN

THE MINOR PROPHETS

These prophecies were brief and could be written on a single scroll. That is why they are grouped together. The larger ones (e.g., Isaiah, Jeremiah, Ezekiel) had to have a scroll of their own.

Of the writers who have commented on each of the twelve short canonical works, we will mention only two. James Montgomery Boice and H. A. Ironside. Dr. Boice's *The Minor Prophets* (2 volumes) contains his sermons preached before the congregation of the Tenth Avenue Presbyterian Church, Philadelphia. The coverage is excellent.

Dr. Ironside wrote *The Minor Prophets* with the needs of the lay person in mind. The theme of each prophet's book is laid out in such a manner that it can be grasped even if the reader has little previous acquaintance with prophecy.

For those who desire a more detailed discussion, we recommend the following:

THE WISDOM OF THE AGES

Hosea

Derek Kidner's *The Message of Hosea* (The Bible Speaks Today), is an interpretative commentary which places emphasis on God's love for Israel. Kidner sees this being fulfilled at the end of the present age.

Joel

Ronald B. Allen's *Joel*, in the Bible Study Commentary series, deftly intertwines Joel's predictions with material in the book of Acts and the book of Revelation. The result is a work of merit that explains for readers what Joel predicted and how it fits in with other parts of Scripture. The net result is that the reader comes away with an enhanced understanding of what God plans to do.

Amos

J. A. Motyer, in *The Message of Amos* (The Bible Speaks Today), re-examines the message of Amos, the "farmer" from Tekoa, and relates its teaching to the present. Motyer is a fine evangelical, but he fails to come to terms with Israel's future and so tends to apply the text directly to the church.

Obadiah

Before his death the late Frank E. Gaebelein combined four individual, previously written studies on different prophets into a single book. The result, entitled *Four Minor Prophets: Obadiah, Jonah, Habakkuk, and Haggai*, is refreshing because Dr. Gaebelein was not a trained theologian and so did not write out of a pre-set mold. Here is a book from which all lay people can profit.

Jonah

There are numerous good studies on the book of Jonah. Samuel C. Burn's *The Prophet Jonah* is one of the most satisfactory works to have been written on this Old Testament prophet. And Robert T. Kendall's *Jonah: An Exposition* is an example of expository preaching at its best.

Thomas Kirk's *Jonah: His Life and Time* is a devout presentation of the way in which God the Father sought to bring Jonah, His recalcitrant son, into a satisfying relationship with Himself. O. S. Hawkins is a popular Southern Baptist pastor. His *Jonah: Meeting the God of the Second Chance* is an example of a homiletic commentary that is also devotional and written in the best evangelical tradition. He never hedges on important issues, and succeeds in giving to Christian lay people an uplifting exposition that will edify their souls.

Micah

Jack R. Riggs' *Micah* (Bible Study Commentary) sorts through the interpretive difficulties of this book and succeeds in explaining in lay people's terms the meaning and message of Micah.

Nahum

There are few good commentaries on the book of Nahum, and John R. Kohlenberger's *Jonah and Nahum* (Everyman's Bible Commentary series) is included here for the sake of completeness. He makes available a verse-by-verse exposition of these two books that have as their common focal point the ancient city of Nineveh. He readily reveals the practical value of these prophetic writings.

Habakkuk

We have already commented on some books that contain an exposition of more than one of the Minor Prophets. To this may be added *Habakkuk and Zephaniah* (Everyman's Bible Commentary) by C. J. Barber. This is a clear, non-technical exposition that opens up the problems of injustice and suffering on the one hand and God's plan for the consummation of the age on the other.

Zephaniah

The best, substantive work to appear in recent years is Ronald B. Allen's *A Shelter in the Fury*. It is a popularly written commentary that explains the "key" Zephaniah had discerned whereby Israel would be able to withstand the "Day of the Lord." Other emphases associated with this message of hope are the avoidance of God's wrath and His love for Israel.

Also see above under Habakkuk.

Haggai

Herbert Wolf's *Haggai and Malachi* (Everyman's Bible Commentary) reveals the timeliness and relevance of these prophetic writings. His writing style is clear and he is able to communicate the nuances of the Hebrew text without becoming technical. This is a most helpful treatment.

Zechariah

Charles L. Feinberg's popular *God Remembers: A Study of Zechariah* possesses an enduring quality. His competent handling of even the most difficult prophetic visions gives readers confidence, and his interweaving of material from other prophecies enables him to apply the message of Zechariah with unerring precision.

Malachi

Walter C. Kaiser, Jr., wrote a commentary on Malachi that he hoped would become a prototype for a whole new series. We trust that it will. *Malachi: God's Unchanging Love* contains

all that makes a commentary worthwhile. This is a work that
can be read with profit by a lay person as well as pastor. It is
highly recommended.

And finally, John A. Oswalt's *Where Are You, God?* is designed to help people in our modern milieu cope with a civilization that has run amok and is unsure of how to get out of
the mess it's in.

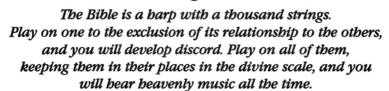

The Bible is a harp with a thousand strings.
Play on one to the exclusion of its relationship to the others,
and you will develop discord. Play on all of them,
keeping them in their places in the divine scale, and you
will hear heavenly music all the time.

WILLIAM P WHITE.

CHAPTER 5

OUR LEGACY

*Reading is to the mind, what exercise is to the body. As by
the one, health is preserved, strengthened, and invigorated;
by the other, virtue, which is the health of the mind, is kept
alive, cherished, and confirmed.*

JOSEPH ADDISON

A national Bible quiz was given to high school seniors several years ago. They were anticipating entering a Christian
college, and the accrediting agency was bringing pressure to
bear upon the administration of the college to reduce the Bible
requirements. There were one hundred questions that could
be answered with a brief, one sentence response. Here are a
few of the questions with the most common responses (MCR)
given by the students:

Q.:   **Who were Matthew, Mark, and Luke?**
MCR: The brothers of Jesus.
Q.:   **Where was Jesus born?**
MCR: South America.
Q.:   **Name two of the people to whom Paul wrote
       letters.**
MCR: Priscilla and Thyatira (in the majority of instances
       the names were spelled incorrectly).
Q.:   **Which was the first gospel to be written?**
MCR: The one to the Hebrews.

The average grade was 10% with the highest being 34%.

The Life of Christ

Foremost in the study of the New Testament is the life and work of Jesus Christ. While many books have been written about Him, we will confine ourselves to just three, with a fourth work focusing attention on those with whom He had contact during His ministry.

First, there is Robert D. Culver's *The Life of Christ*. Dr. Culver is a fine theologian. He is one of those whose skills have gone unrecognized for too long. He does not fit any preconceived mold, and yet everything he says or writes about has the ring of truth to it. All this applies to his concise, well-reasoned book *The Life of Christ*. The text is enhanced with photographs, maps, and diagrams. It is an excellent place at which to begin one's study of the New Testament.

Second, there is J. Dwight Pentecost's *The Words and Works of Jesus Christ*. Dr. Pentecost is less original but follows an important thematic approach to the life of Christ borrowed from Matthew's gospel. This stands in contrast to many older works that treat Christ's ministry geographically. His account of what the Lord Jesus said and did may well be regarded as indispensable!

Then, of a different nature, there is G. Campbell Morgan's *The Crisis of the Christ*. It focuses attention on the major turning points of Christ's ministry. Wilbur M. Smith wrote:

> I think this is the most important single volume that Dr. Morgan ever wrote. It is a masterpiece. It is a study of the Incarnation, the Baptism, the Temptation, the Transfiguration, the Crucifixion, the Resurrection and the Ascension.

Dr. Morgan's companion volume, *The Great Physician*, is likewise worthy of your careful consideration. It narrows the field to those individuals with whom Christ had contact during His brief sojourn on earth. Like light radiating from a sparkling diamond, so this work shows the reactions of different people to the ministry of the Son of God. Some were converted, and their lives were forever changed. Others came to Him or were brought to Him, and were healed of their illness. Some came, saw their need, but went away sorrowful. And a few plotted His death. It's all here in these well-told stories.

— 🕭 —

After six years given to the impartial investigation
of Christianity as to its truth or falsity,
I have come to the deliberate conclusion that Jesus Christ
is the Messiah of the Jews, the Savior of the world,
and my personal Savior.

LEW WALLACE AUTHOR OF *BEN HUR*

— 🕭 —

A Guide to the Gospels

There are many introductory works highlighting the unique contents of the gospels. One of the most satisfactory is W. Graham Scroggie's *Guide to the Gospels*. When I was in seminary I was told: "This one book is worth a whole shelf of books on the same subject." Over the years I have found that to be correct.

Harmony of the Gospels

In time you will want to take note of those places where Matthew, Mark, and Luke (called the Synoptic gospels) share a similar content. Also of interest is where one or the other adds material not found in the other two.

The most reliable source for this kind of material is Robert L. Thomas and Stanley N. Gundry's *A Harmony of the Gospels*. It is well outlined, and the text is in parallel columns to make crossreference easy. In the back of the book there are important essays discussing different approaches to the interpretation of the text, as well as its history, chronology, and much more. This *Harmony* is available for a variety of translations (NASB, NKJV, and NIV).

— 🐚 —

As we consider some of the best lay-level commentaries on each book of the New Testament, let us not forget that Charles R. Erdman, H. A. Ironside, and Warren W. Wiersbe have given us commentaries on each canonical book.

Matthew

Stanley D. Toussaint's *Behold the King* is based upon a thorough knowledge of the Greek text, yet it can be read with ease by the average lay person. Its approach to Christ's life is thematic, and this immediately sheds fresh light on all the Lord Jesus said and did.

Also worthy of your serious consideration is John F. Walvoord's *Matthew: Thy Kingdom Come*. Dr. Walvoord takes his readers step by step through the events Matthew recorded, interpreting them in light of Christ's offer of the kingdom and its rejection by the leaders of the people. In this book we have the expertise of a great theologian giving to those younger in the faith a legacy that will last for a lifetime.

Mark

Robert Alan Cole has recently updated his practical and helpful 1961 edition of *The Gospel of Mark: An Introduction and Commentary* (Tyndale New Testament Commentaries). While the new Introduction is designed more for the pastor or seminary student, the comments on the text continue to meet the needs of lay people. For many years this work has remained one of the best treatments for the average reader, and we are gratified to know that its place is assured for at least the next thirty years.

For a delightful blend of scholarship and devotion you must read D. Edmond Hiebert's *Mark: A Portrait of the Servant. The Minister's Library* (II: 124) called it "a reverent and insightful treatment." While other works are more flamboyant, this one is solid and reliable. It repays careful reading.

Finally, Ray C. Stedman's *The Servant Who Rules* (Mark 1:1–8:26) and *The Ruler Who Serves* (Mark 8:27–16:20) presents Christ as the believer's role model. Through the unfolding of each scene the author shows Him to be the fulfillment of Isaiah's teaching on the Servant of Jehovah.

Luke

Frederic L. Godet is a writer who deserves our respect. He never knowingly sidestepped an interpretative problem. His writings reveal a devout spirit coupled with his thorough familiarity with the text. His *Gospel of Luke* is one of the best commentaries ever written on this portion of God's Word.

Because of certain attacks against the virginal conception of the Lord Jesus, a capable handling of the birth narrative is essential. Leon Morris' *The Gospel According to St. Luke* (Tyndale New Testament Commentaries) reflects real maturity in his defense of the faith. All things considered, this is a most helpful volume to have in one's home.

John

Expositions of John's gospel are both numerous and diverse. James Montgomery Boice has given us *The Gospel of John*. The contents consists of messages delivered to the congregation Dr. Boice pastors in Philadelphia. The timeliness and relevance of his material is encapsulated in the following excerpt from a review published in *Bibliotheca Sacra*: "Any expositor, beginner or veteran, will find this work useful not only in the realm of interpretation but also in applications, illustrations, and quotations."

Another helpful work is by Homer A. Kent, Jr. It's title, appropriately, is *Light in the Darkness*. Dr. Kent surveys the contents of John's gospel paragraph by paragraph. His style bears the mark of the classroom, and yet there is a devotional content to all that is included in his book.

And then there is John Phillips' *Exploring the Gospels: John*. It places before lay Bible students a well-organized, evangelical explanation of the text. Dr. Phillips does not spend much time on problems of interpretation, but what is here is worth reading.

— 𝕬 —

The habit of reading ... is your pass[port]
to the greatest, the purest, and the most perfect
pleasures that God has prepared for His creatures....
It lasts when other pleasures fade.
ANTHONY TROLLOPE

— 𝕬 —

The Acts of the Apostles

We tend to forget that the first churches met in houses. By way of reminder there is F. F. Bruce's *The Acts of the Apostles* (New International Commentary on the New Testament, Revised edition). When compared with the very popular 1954 edition, this work shows slight changes and a few additions. The introductory material has been updated and the bibliographies are more extensive. Otherwise there is the same solid, lucid exposition people have relied on for the past 40 years.

G. Campbell Morgan's *The Acts of the Apostles* was at one time regarded as the most important single expository work for the pastor. But this is not entirely accurate. Dr. Morgan's treatment is equally as valuable for the lay person, and his recounting of the events that took the early church from provincial Jerusalem to cosmopolitan Rome, is exceedingly well done. Sunday school and home Bible class teachers will profit greatly from Dr. Morgan's competent handling of the text.

Charles C. Ryrie, who has given us the *Ryrie Study Bible*, also wrote commentaries on several New Testament books.

His *Acts of the Apostles* (in the Everyman Bible Study series) contains a brief, helpful discussion of the issues. Where this work shines is in his treatment of the transitional nature of Acts showing how a predominantly Jewish church gradually gave way to a predominantly Gentile one.

And not to be overlooked in a day of theological confusion is John R. W. Stott's *The Spirit, the Church, and the World*. The exposition proceeds on a verse-by-verse basis, and Dr. Stott provides his readers with a good discussion of the issues. He possesses the ability to blend history and matters arising out of his careful exegesis into a highly readable, informative exposition.

> Even the apostle Paul knew the value of reading good books. When imprisoned again, he wrote to Timothy and said: "Make every effort to come to me soon....When you come bring...the books, especially the parchments" (2 Timothy 4:9,13).

The Apostle Paul

An enormous body of literature has grown up around the life and ministry of the apostle Paul. One of the most fluid, easy-to-read books of recent years has come from the pen, not of a theologian, but of an Oxford scholar named Ernle Bradford who for more than twenty years captained a ship in the Mediterranean. Entitled *Paul the Traveller*, the book traces the journeys of the apostle Paul, the places he visited, and the people to whom he ministered.

Other works can be traced through *The Minister's Library*, Volume I:194-198 and Volume II: 135-138.

Some important books discuss the contribution of those who labored with Paul in different parts of the Roman Empire. The best is D. Edmond Hiebert's *Personalities Around Paul*. This is a superb discussion of those who labored with the apostle and furthered the work of the local church. It also delineates the nature and character of Paul's opponents.

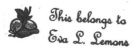

Romans

As we turn to the epistles we once again have occasion to refer to a book by F. F. Bruce. This one, entitled *The Letter of Paul to the Romans* (Tyndale New Testament Commentaries, Revised edition), is a brief exposition of this letter and is based on solid exegesis.

Another solid and reliable work is Frederic L. Godet's *Commentary on Romans*. Dr. Godet's comments on the text come from his years of reflection on the meaning and message of this important Epistle. As a result, readers will find much that is unique in this exposition.

On a more popular level there is R. Kent Hughes' book, *Romans: Righteousness from Heaven* in the Preaching the Word series. It is a very readable, homiletic commentary, and there is evidence throughout of Dr. Hughes' desire to minister to the needs of people. The result is a high degree of relevancy that makes this volume ideal for use in home Bible study groups.

The Corinthian Epistles

Robert G. Gromacki's *Called To Be Saints* and *Stand Firm in the Faith* cover First and Second Corinthians. Dr. Gromacki sticks rigidly to the biblical text and expounds the central theme of each Epistle with clarity and insight. At no time does he become obtuse, nor does he obliquely sidestep difficult issues. Readers will find that he explains technical matters in a non-technical way.

Another book that is worthy of serious consideration is Philip E. Hughes' *Paul's Second Epistle to the Corinthians* (New International Commentary on the New Testament). This is a substantive work, and it is without question one of the best conservative commentaries to have been written on Second Corinthians. Dr. Hughes writes without ostentation. He leads his readers through Paul's second letter, explaining the background and exhorting believers to heed the apostle's counsel.

A work devoted to an analysis of the first letter is Robert B.

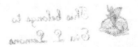

Hughes' *First Corinthians* (Everyman Bible Commentary). It is as capable and concise a commentary as one can find. Dr. Hughes deals adequately with all the important issues and succeeds in combining substance with a pleasing literary style.

Then there is Ray C. Stedman's *Expository Studies in 2 Corinthians*. Dr. Stedman defends the church as an organism within God's economy, and points to those things that will help it achieve the purpose God intended. This is a most valuable treatise.

Finally, there is Robert L. Thomas' *Understanding Spiritual Gifts*—an exposition of 1 Corinthians chapters 12–14. While more scholarly than any of the other books mentioned thus far, Dr. Thomas' discussion is so pertinent to the needs of the church, readers should put forth the effort to master all he has to say.

Galatians

William Barclay provided us with a timely examination of Galatians 5:19-23 in *Flesh and Spirit*. His word studies of each term used by the apostle expand our understanding of Paul's thought while causing us to come to a new appreciation of the riches that can be uncovered though the study of words.

In addition, we are again indebted to Robert Alan Cole for his lucid *Letter of Paul to the Galatians* (Tyndale New Testament Commentary, Revised edition). Not only does he instruct us about what Paul wrote, he also informs us of the charter of our liberty. This is a timely book on an important subject. It should not be neglected.

Homer A. Kent, Jr. has written on *The Freedom of God's Sons*. It is a well-outlined treatment of Paul's theme, and manifests a capable handling of those verses that have given rise to interpretative difficulties throughout the history of the Christian church.

John R. W. Stott's writings have always been well received,

and they seldom fail to inspire and encourage believers in their walk. In his slender volume, *The Message of Galatians* (The Bible Speaks Today), he lays out the meaning of the letter to the Galatians in terms that lay people can appreciate and understand.

Ephesians

R. Kent Hughes' *Ephesians: The Mystery of the Body of Christ* (Preaching the Word) is clear, concise, and convincing. His writing style flows, and there is throughout a captivating devotional emphasis. Dr. Hughes both teaches and edifies at the same time, and this treatment of Ephesians will be welcomed by all who read this book.

Also of value is *Ephesians* by John F. MacArthur, Jr. (MacArthur New Testament Commentary series). The author is in the process of providing a commentary on the entire New Testament. Several books have multiple volumes (e.g., Matthew with four volumes). Dr. MacArthur is theologically precise; and he deals convincingly with the mystery of Christ's body, and of the believer's vital union with his/her risen Lord in Heaven.

To the list of books by John Phillips we must add one more, *Exploring Ephesians*. A lot of thought went into the production of the manuscript, and throughout there is evidence of Dr. Phillips' thoroughness. His material is illustrated with quotations and poems, and he expounds the text with vigor born of confidence and a lifetime of study.

Ray C. Stedman's *Spiritual Warfare* is must reading for every Christian. Basing his counsel on Ephesians 6:10-17, he challenges believers to avail themselves of "the whole armor of God." At the same time he exposes the false emphases on Satanism and demonism in the church. The importance of this book cannot be overstated. It should be among the first a Christian reads as he begins the second year of his Christian life. And it should be reread at regular intervals thereafter.

John R. W. Stott's *God's New Society: The Message of Ephesians* (The Bible Speaks Today), should also be placed high on a believer's priority list. Bible class teachers will find here an example of expository preaching at its best. Its message is vital to the church's well-being.

Philippians

Of recent works on this Epistle there is J. Dwight Pentecost's *The Joy of Living*. These chapters by Dr. Pentecost not only do justice to the apostle's stated purpose, they also enlighten and edify the reader as he or she is led in a study of the text by this master expositor.

Another work of real merit is Lehman Strauss' *Devotional Studies in Philippians*. Within the covers of this book the reader is treated to a delightful, well-outlined series of meditations.

And then there is Kenneth S. Wuest's *Philippians in the Greek New Testament*. The treatment is nontechnical, so do not be put off by the title. Dr. Wuest does not clutter the page with Greek words or phrases, but transliterates the words to which he refers and explains word meanings in ways that elucidate the intent of the Biblical writer. This commentary can be read and enjoyed by those with no knowledge of the original language. The same is true of all his writings.

Colossians

R. Kent Hughes' *Colossians and Philemon: The Supremacy of Christ*, is similar to his other works on the New Testament. His style is impressive, and he succeeds in relating the uniqueness of Christ's provision to the needs of individual believers.

The work by W. H. Griffith Thomas, *Studies in Colossians and Philemon*, is a gem. Dr. Thomas had a pleasing homiletical style, and the information he includes is provocative and results in the reader's edification.

The Thessalonian Epistles

One of the best overall study of these letters is D. Edmond Hiebert's *The Thessalonian Epistles*. It was out of print for a time, but it has recently been reissued. Dr. Hiebert is a devout Christian and consistently maintains high standards in all he does. His study of these early letters of Paul sets a standard for accuracy and reliability.

Another helpful work is Charles C. Ryrie's *The Epistles to the Thessalonians*. Though brief, Dr. Ryrie makes his point in his seemingly effortless manner.

Frederick A. Tatford's *Paul's Letters to the Thessalonians* was written when the author was in his eighties and published posthumously. This slender volume combines information drawn from Dr. Tatford's travels in Greece with his exposition of the text. This verse-by-verse commentary not only unfolds the teachings of these Epistles, but also underscores the believer's hope as well.

The Pastoral Epistles

Donald Guthrie revised *The Pastoral Epistles* which was first issued in 1957. His coverage of the information Paul wanted to communicate to Timothy and Titus includes a rebuttal of the theories of those who have disputed Paul's authorship and denied the unity of the composition of these letters. The exposition of the text is easily understood, and what Dr. Guthrie presents is admirably suited for lay use.

D. Edmond Hiebert has given us three small though adequate monographs entitled *First Timothy, Second Timothy,* and *Titus and Philemon*. Each work is a masterpiece of condensed information, and we are grateful that this material is readily available.

Homer A. Kent's *The Pastoral Epistles* (Revised edition), has some unique features. He boldly champions the Pauline authorship of each letter, and then provides an exemplary exposition of it. Lay people will find that Dr. Kent is a master in the art of communicating what needs to be known.

Finally, John R. W. Stott has given us an authoritative work on Second Timothy entitled *Guard the Gospel*. His many gifts are put to good use as he ties in Paul's teaching with the needs of the present day. Here is a model of the kind of succinct, relevant Biblical scholarship towards which we should all strive.

Philemon

The works of Samuel Cox and A. H. Drysdale entitled *The Epistle to Philemon* are combined to give the Bible class teacher or Christian worker an adequate understanding of this New Testament "postcard." No one can read what these dedicated men of God have written and remain unmoved.

W. Graham Scroggie's *Studies in Philemon* is possibly the best exposition ever written in this short book.

Other books on this letter can be traced by consulting the commentaries on Colossians.

Hebrews

Among the standard treatments is F. F. Bruce's *The Epistle to the Hebrews* (New International Commentary on the New Testament, Revised edition). First issued in 1964, this commentary has been the mainstay of evangelicals for the past three decades. Dr. Bruce's treatment of Old Testament quotations used by the writer of Hebrews, is most helpful. His discussions of the supremacy of Christ over Old Testaments roles and rituals is likewise of great value.

Donald Guthrie's *The Letter to the Hebrews* (Tyndale New Testament commentaries series) interprets the letter as having been addressed to Jews who were in danger of apostasizing back into Judaism. His overall treatment is helpful. If there is a lack it occurs in his handling of those "problem passages" that have caused concern among gentile Christians studying this Epistle.

Another book from the "top drawer" is Philip E. Hughes' masterful *A Commentary on the Epistle to the Hebrews*. It is such an outstanding work it deserves a place among the foremost expositions on Hebrews. Dr. Hughes marshals his facts and presents them with conviction born of long exposure to the text of the New Testament in general, and of the letter to the Hebrews in particular.

James

D. Edmond Hiebert's exposition of *The Epistle of James: Tests of a Living Faith*, not only explains the intent of the writer, but also shows his unity of purpose. Dr. Hiebert never gives his reader the impression that he is in a hurry. But neither does he linger too long over a particular subject. His balance is remarkable, and his style is such that his work is readable without becoming tedious.

Lehman Strauss has penned a work that bears the title of *James Your Brother*. It is an evangelical commentary that, for the most part, avoids controversial issues, and succeeds in providing devotional thoughts on the text. These warm the heart and enrich the soul.

The Epistles of Peter

Once again D. Edmond Hiebert has done yeoman work to give us two books: *First Peter*, and *Second Peter and Jude*. In them he provides a verse-by-verse study with discussions of Greek words and terms. His work is so exemplary one is left with the feeling that he has set a standard of excellence toward which others should strive. These are fine expositions, and it is hoped that many will avail themselves of them.

Robert Leighton's *A Practical Commentary Upon the First Epistle of Peter* is one of the best expositions on First Peter. Dr. Leighton provides his readers with the results of his vast learning without ostentation. His theology is accurate, and his eloquence unmatched.

Two older works that are of more worth to lay people than their replacements are Alan M. Stibbs" *The First Epistle General of Peter* and E. M. B. Green's *The Second Epistle General of Peter and The General Epistle of Jude*. Stibbs' treatment of the text of First Peter is in the finest evangelical tradition, and Green's handling of Second Peter and Jude is based on detailed exegesis. Both writers apply the teaching of these Epistles to the needs of believers today.

The Johannine Epistles

Good commentaries on John's letters are plentiful. D. Edmond Hiebert's *The Epistles of John* is one of the best. He carefully follows John's cyclical thought and succeeds in bringing out the meaning of the text.

Lehman Strauss' *The Epistles of John* appears to have been patterned after Robert Law's *The Tests of Life*. Most of the verses are covered. Dr. Strauss includes in his book some usable illustrations that lay teachers and preachers may find helpful .

John R. W. Stott's *The Epistles of John* (Revised edition) deserves to be marked with an asterisk, for it is one of the most satisfactory commentaries to have been written on John's letters. Dr. Stott combines a knowledge of the needs of the local church with the truths that the apostle John felt were desperately needed by believers of every age.

The Epistle of Jude

Many years ago S. Maxwell Coder authored *The Acts of the Apostates*, and although his style is now dated, this remains an important study of this long-neglected Epistle.

John F. MacArthur, Jr. has given us *Beware of Pretenders*, in which he applies the teaching of Jude in ways that meet the needs of contemporary Christians.

Frederick A. Tatford has enhanced our understanding of the historic events which gave rise to Jude's Epistle in *Jude's Apostates* (published in England by Upperton Press). Dr. Tatford ties in Jude's teaching with the needs of the church and lays bare the character of those whose false teaching was leading some believers to engage in immorality and other forms of lawlessness.

Revelation

William Barclay wrote two books on the seven letters to the churches of Asia (Revelation 1–3). One carries the title *Letters to the Seven Churches*, and the other is Volume 1 of *The Revelation of John* in his *Daily Bible Studies* series. The two volumes have different contents. They are, however, complimentary. In each the exposition is based on a careful re-creation of the historic setting of the first century A.D.—the worship associated with the pagan religions, and the very real threat to believers of persecution. Each letter has been subjected to the author's usual careful scrutiny, and together these books provide a discerning analysis of what Christ thought of His first century church.

Leon Morris approaches the book of Revelation from an amillennial perspective. His work, entitled *The Book of Revelation* (Tyndale New Testament Commentaries. Revised edition), is concise and shows the breadth and depth of his understanding of apocalyptic literature.

The most satisfying work for general use is John F. Walvoord's *The Revelation of Jesus Christ*. It is also a companion volume to his study on Daniel. Dr. Walvoord follows a consistent, literal interpretation. He leads the reader through a panorama of what will happen during the tribulation period, and culminates with a description of the eternal state.

*Books must be read as deliberately and reservedly
as they were written.*

HENRY DAVID THOREAU

BIBLIOGRAPHY

— ❧ —

Adeney, Walter F. *Ezra and Nehemiah.* Grand Rapids: Kregel Publications, 1980.

Aharoni, Yohanan, and Michael Avi-Yonah. *The Macmillan Bible Atlas* (Third edition. Edited by A. F. Rainey and Z. Safrai) New York: Macmillan Co., 1993.

Alexander, Joseph A. *Isaiah, Translated and Explained.* Grand Rapids: Kregel Publications, 1992.

Alexander, Ralph. *Ezekiel.*Chicago: Moody Press, 1979.

Allen, Ronald B. *Joel.* Bible Study Commentary. Grand Rapids: Zondervan Publishing House, 1988.

_____. *A Shelter in the Fury.* Portland, OR: Multnomah, 1986.

Anderson, Francis I. *Job.* Tyndale OT Commentaries. Downer's Grove, IL: InterVarsity Press, 1976.

Arnot, William. *Studies in Proverbs.* Grand Rapids: Kregel Publications, 1978.

Baldwin, Joyce G. *1 and 2 Samuel.* Tyndale O.T. Commentaries, Volume 8. Downers Grove, IL: InterVarsity Press, 1989.

Barber, Cyril J. *The Minister's Library.* 2 volumes. Neptune, NJ: Loizeaux, 1974, 1987.

_____. *Judges: A Narrative of God's Power.* Neptune, NJ: Loizeaux, 1990.

_____. *Ruth: A Story of God's Grace.* Neptune, NJ: Loizeaux, 1989.

_____. *The Books of Samuel,* 2 Volumes. Neptune, NJ: Loizeaux, 1994, 2000.

_____. *Nehemiah, and the Dynamics of Effective Leadership.* Neptune, NJ: Loizeaux, 1991.

_____. *Habakkuk and Zephaniah.* Everyman's Bible Commentary. Chicago: Moody Press, 1984.

Barclay, William. *Daily Study Bible: New Testament* 18 Volumes. Belleville, MI: Westminster/John Knox Press, 1979.

_____. *Flesh and Spirit.* Nashville: Abingdon, 1962.

_____. *Letters to the Seven Churches.* Belleville, MI: Westminster/ John Knox Press, 1982.

_____. *Revelation of John,* Volume 1. Daily Study Bible. Belleville, MI.: Westminster/John Knox Press, 1976.

Baxter, J. Sidlow. *Explore the Book.* Grand Rapids: Zondervan Publishing House, 1986.

Beitzel, Barry J. *The Moody Altas of Bible Lands.* Chicago: Moody Press, 1985.

Blaikie, William G. *The Book of Joshua.* Grand Rapids: Kregel Publications, 1978.

_____. *The First Book of Samuel.* Grand Rapids: Kregel Publications, 1978.

_____. *The Second Book of Samuel.* Grand Rapids: Kregel Publications, 1978.

Boice, James M. *The Gospel of John.* Grand Rapids: Zondervan Publishing House, 1985.

_____. *The Minor Prophets*. 2 volumes. Grand Rapids: Zondervan Publishing House, 1988.

Bradford, Ernle. *Paul the Traveller*. New York: Macmillan Co., 1977.

Bruce, F.F. *The Acts of the Apostles*. New International Commentary on the New Testament. Revised Edition. Grand Rapids: Wm. B. Eerdmans Pub. Co., 1989.

_____. *The Letter of Paul to the Romans*. Tyndale N. T. Commentaries, Revised Edition. Grand Rapids: Wm. B. Eerdmans Pub. Co., 1985.

_____. *The Epistle to the Hebrews*. New International Commentary on the New Testament, Revised Edition. Grand Rapids: Wm. B. Eerdmans Pub. Co., 1990.

Burn, Samuel C. *The Prophet Jonah*. Grand Rapids: Kregel Publications, 1981.

Bush, George. *Commentary on Exodus*. Grand Rapids: Kregel Publications, 1993.

_____. *Notes on Leviticus*. Grand Rapids: Kregel Publications, 1981.

_____. *Notes on Judges*. Grand Rapids: Kregel Publications, 1976.

Cairns, Earle E. *Christianity Through the Centuries*. Grand Rapids: Zondervan Publishing House, 1981.

Carr, G. Lloyd. *The Song of Solomon*. Tyndale O.T. Commentaries, Volume 17. Downers Grove, IL: InterVarsity Press, 1984.

Coder, S. Maxwell. *The Acts of the Apostates*. Chicago: Moody Press, 1958.

Cole, Robert Allan. *Exodus: An Introduction and Commentary*. Tyndale O.T. Commentaries. Downers Grove, IL: InterVarsity Press, 1979.

_____. *The Gospel of Mark: An Introduction and Commentary.* Tyndale N.T. Commentaries. Downer's Grove, IL: InterVarsity Press, 1961.

_____. *Letter of Paul to the Galatians.* Tyndale N.T. Commentaries. Downer's Grove, IL: InterVarsity Press, 1965.

Cox, Samuel and A. H. Drysdale. *The Epistle to Philemon.* Grand Rapids: Kregel Publications, 1982.

Culver, Robert D. *Daniel and the Latter Days.* Chicago: Moody Press, 1954.

_____. *The Life of Christ.* Grand Rapids: Baker Book House, 1976.

Cundall, Arthur E. and Leon Morris. *Judges and Ruth.* Tyndale O.T. Commentaries. Downers Grove, IL: InterVarsity Press, 1979.

Davis, John J. *Paradise to Prison: Studies in Genesis.* Winona Lake, Ind.: BMH Books, 1979; and Grand Rapids: Baker Book House/ Revell, 1979.

Enns, Paul P. *The Moody Handbook of Theology.* Chicago: Moody Press, 1989.

_____. *Joshua.* Bible Study Commentary Series. Grand Rapids: Zondervan Publishing House, 1981.

_____. *Ezekiel.* Bible Study Commentary Series. Grand Rapids: Zondervan Publishing House, 1986.

Erdman, Charles R. *The Book of Deuteronomy: An Exposition.* Grand Rapids: Baker Book House, 1982.

_____. *The Book of Numbers: An Exposition.* Grand Rapids: Baker Book House, 1982.

_____. *Commentary on the New Testament* 17 Volumes.

_____. *Jeremiah and Lamentations: An Exposition.* Grand Rapids: Baker Book House,

Feinberg, Charles L. *God Remembers: A Study of Zecharaiah.*

_____. *Jeremiah, A Commentary.* Grand Rapids: Zondervan Publishing House, 1982.

Gaebelein, Arno C. *Gaebelein's Concise Commentary on the Whole Bible.* Neptune: Loizeaux, 1985.

_____. *Four Minor Prophets: Obadiah, Jonah, Habakkuk, and Haggai.* Neptune: Loizeaux.

Geisler, Norman L. and William E. Nix. *A General Introduction to the Bible.* Chicago: Moody Press, 1979.

Glickman, S. Craig. *A Song for Lovers.* Downers Grove, IL: InterVarsity Press, 1979.

Godet, Frederic L. *Gospel of Luke.* Grand Rapids: Zondervan Publishing House, n.d.

_____. *Commentary on Romans.* Grand Rapids: Kregel Publications, 1979.

Goodrich, E. W. and John R. Kohlenberger, III, editors. *The NIV Complete Concordance.* Grand Rapids: Zondervan Publishing House, 1981.

Green, E. M. B. *The Second Epistle General of Peter and the General Epistle of Jude.* Grand Rapids: Wm. B. Eerdmans Pub. Co., 1968.

Green, Jay, editor. *The Interlinear Hebrew/Greek English Bible.* Grand Rapids: Baker Book House, 1976.

Gromacki, Robert G. *Called To Be Saints.* Grand Rapids: Baker Book House, 1977.

_____. *Stand Firm in the Faith*. Grand Rapids: Baker Book House: 1979.

Guthrie, Donald. *The Pastoral Epistles*. Grand Rapids: Wm. B. Eerdmans Publishing Co., 1991.

_____. *The Letter to the Hebrews*. Tyndale N.T. Commentaries. Grand Rapids: Wm. B. Eerdmans Publishing Co., 1983

Hamilton, Victor P. *Handbook on the Pentateuch*. Grand Rapids: Baker Book House/ Revell, 1982.

Harrison, Roland K. *Leviticus, An Introduction and Commentary*. Tyndale O.T. Commentaries. Downers Grove, IL: InterVarsity Press, 1980.

_____. *Jeremiah and Lamentations*. Downers Grove, IL: InterVarsity Press, 1979.

Harrison, R. K., Howard F. Vos, Cyril J. Barber, and editors. *New Ungers Bible Dictionary*. Chicago: Moody Press, 1984.

Hawkins, O.S. *Jonah: Meeting the God of the Second Chance*. Neptune, NJ: Loizeaux, 1990.

Hendricks, Howard G. and William Hendricks. *Living by the Book*. Chicago: Moody Press, 1991.

Hiebert, D. Edmond. *The Epistles of James: Tests of a Living Faith*. Chicago: Moody Press, 1979.

_____. *The Epistles of John*. Greenville, SC: Bob Jones University Press, 1991.

_____. *First Peter*. Chicago: Moody Press, 1984.

_____. *First Timothy*. Chicago: Moody Press, 1979.

_____. *Mark: A Portrait of the Servant*. Chicago: Moody Press, 1974.

_____. *Personalities Around Paul.* Chicago: Moody Press, 1973.

_____. *Second Peter and Jude.* Greenville, S.C.: Bob Jones University Press, 1989.

_____. *Second Timothy.* Chicago: Moody Press, 1979.

_____. *The Thessalonian Epistles.* Chicago: Moody Press, 1971.

_____. *Titus and Philemon.* Chicago: Moody Press, 1979.

Hughes, Philip E. *A Commentary on the Epistle to the Hebrews.* Grand Rapids: Wm. B. Eerdmans Publishing Co., 1987.

_____. *Paul's Second Epistle to the Corinthians.* Grand Rapids: Wm. B. Eerdmans Publishing Co., 1962.

Hughes, R. Kent. *Colossians and Philemon: The Supremacy of Christ.* Wheaton, IL: Crossway Books, 1989.

_____. *Ephesians: The Mystery of the Body of Christ.* Wheaton, IL: Crossway Books, 1990.

_____. *Romans: Righteousness from Heaven.* Wheaton, IL: Crossway Books, 1991.

Hughes, Robert B. *First Corinthians.* Chicago: Moody Press, 1985.

Ironside, H. A. Commentary Series. Neptune, NJ: Loizeaux.

Kaiser, Walter C., Jr. *A Biblical Approach to Personal Suffering.* Chicago: Moody Press, 1982.

_____. *Ecclesiastes: Total Life.* Chicago: Moody Press, 1979.

_____. *Malachi: God's Unchanging Love.* Grand Rapids: Baker Book House, 1984.

Kelly, William. *An Exposition of the Book of Isaiah*. Grand Rapids: Kregel Publications, 1979.

Kendall, Robert T. *Jonah: An Exposition*. Grand Rapids: Zondervan Publishing House, 1978.

Kent, Homer A. Jr., *The Freedom of God's Sons: Studies in Galatians*. Winona Lake, IN: BMH Books, 1979.

_____. *Light in the Darkness: Studies in the Gospel of John*. Winona Lake, IN: BMH Books, 1979.

_____. *The Pastoral Epistles*. Winona Lake, IN: BMH Books, 1982.

Kidner, Derek. *A Time to Mourn, A Time to Dance: Ecclesiastes and the Way of the World*. Downers Grove, IL: InterVarsity Press, 1984.

_____. *The Message of Hosea*. Downers Grove, IL: InterVarsity Press, 1987.

Kirk, Thomas, and George Rawlinson. *Studies in the Books of Kings*. Grand Rapids: Kregel Publications.

Knapp, Christopher. *Kings of Judah and Israel*. Neptune, NJ: Loizeaux,

Kohlenberger, John R. *Jonah and Nahum*. Chicago: Moody Press, 1984.

Lawson, George. *Commentary on Proverbs*. Grand Rapids: Kregel, 1992.

Leighton, Robert. *A Practical Commentary Upon the First Epistle of Peter*. Grand Rapids: Kregel Publications, 1983.

Lightner, Robert P. *Evangelical Theology: A Survey and Review*. Grand Rapids: Baker Book House/ Revell, 1986.

Livingstone, G. H. *The Pentateuch in It's Cultural Environment*. Grand Rapids: Baker Book House/ Revell, 1979.

MacArthur, John F., Jr., *Ephesians*. Chicago: Moody Press, 1985.

_____. *Beware of Pretenders*. Sun Valley, CA: Grace To You, 1990.

Morgan, G. Campbell. *The Acts of the Apostles*. Grand Rapids: Baker Book House/ Revell, 1979.

_____. *The Crisis of the Christ*. Grand Rapids: Baker Book House/ Revell, 1989.

_____. *The Great Physician*. Grand Rapids: Baker Book House/ Revell.

Morris, Leon. *The Gospel According to St. Luke*. Tyndale N.T. Commentaries. Grand Rapids: Wm. B. Eerdmans Publishing Co., 1988.

_____. *The Book of Revelation*. Tyndale N.T. Commentaries. Grand Rapids: Wm. B. Eerdmans Publishing Co., 1987.

Motyer, J. A. *The Message of Amos*. Downers Grove, IL: InterVarsity Press, 1984.

New American Standard Exhaustive Concordance of the Bible. Nashville: Holman Bible Publishers, 1981.

Oswalt, John A. *Where Are You God?* Wheaton, IL: Victor Books, 1982.

Pentecost, J. Dwight. *The Words and Works of Jesus Christ*. Grand Rapids: Zondervan, 1981.

_____. *The Joy of Living: Philippians*. Grand Rapids: Zondervan, 1990.

Perowne, J. J. Stewart. *Commentary on the Psalms*. Grand Rapids: Kregel, 1989.

Phillips, John. *Bible Explorer's Guide*. Neptune, NJ: Loizeaux, 1987.

_____. *Exploring Ephesians*. Neptune, NJ: Loizeaux, 1993.

_____. *Exploring Genesis*. Neptune, NJ: Loizeaux, 1980.

_____. *Exploring the Gospels: John*. Neptune, NJ: Loizeaux, 1989.

_____. *Exploring the Psalms*. 2 Volumes. Neptune, NJ: Loizeaux, 1996.

Phillips, John and Jerry Vines. *Exploring the Book of Daniel*. Neptune, NJ: Loizeaux, 1990.

Raleigh, Alexander. *The Book of Esther*. Grand Rapids: Kregel Publications, 1980.

Rasmussen, Carl. *Zondervan NIV Atlas of the Bible*. Grand Rapids: Zondervan, 1989.

_____. *Micah*. Grand Rapids: Zondervan, 1987.

Ryrie, Charles C. *Acts of the Apostles*. Chicago: Moody Press, 1979.

_____. *Ryrie Study Bible*. Chicago: Moody Press,

_____. *The Epistles to the Thessalonians*. Chicago: Moody Press, 1979.

Sailhamer, John. *1 and 2 Chronicles*. Chicago: Moody Press, 1983.

Scroggie, W. Graham. *Guide to the Gospels*. (Christian Lit. Crusade has *Luke-John* and *Matthew-Mark* 1981).

_____. *Studies in Philemon*. Grand Rapids: Kregel Publications, 1982.

_____. *The Unfolding Drama of Redemption* 3 volumes. London: Pickering and Inglis, 1953-1971.

Schultz, Samuel J. *Deuteronomy: The Gospel of Love*. Chicago: Moody Press, 1979.

Stedman, Ray C. *Expository Studies in 2 Corinthians.* Dallas, TX: Word, 1982.

_____. *The Ruler Who Serves.* Dallas, TX: Word, 1976.

_____. *The Servant Who Rules.* Dallas, TX: Word, 1976.

_____. *Spiritual Warfare.* Portland, OR: Multnomah, 1984.

Stibbs, Alan M. *The First Epistle General of Peter.* Tyndale New Testament Commentaries. Grand Rapids: Wm. B. Eerdmans Pub. Co., 1960.

Stott, John R. W. *God's New Society: The Message of Ephesians.* Downers Grove, IL: InterVarsity Press, 1980.

_____. *Guard the Gospel.* Downer's Grove, IL: InterVarsity Press, 1973.

_____. *The Epistles of John.* Grand Rapids: Wm. B. Eerdmans Pub. Co., 1988.

_____. *The Message of Galatians.* Downer's Grove, IL: InterVarsity Press, 1968.

_____. *The Spirit, the Church, and the World: the Message of Acts.* Downers Grove, IL: InterVarsity Press, 1992.

Strauss, Lehman. *Devotional Studies in Philippians.* Neptune, NJ: Loizeaux, 1959.

_____. *The Epistles of John.* Neptune, NJ: Loizeaux, 1962.

_____. *God's Prophetic Calendar.* Neptune, NJ: Loizeaux. 1987.

_____. *James, Your Brother.* Neptune, NJ: Loizeaux, 1956.

Swindoll, Charles R. *Living on the Ragged Edge.* Nashville: Word Books/ Thomas Nelson, 1987.

Tatford, Frederick A. *Daniel and His Prophecy*. Grand Rapids: Kregel Publications, 1980.

_____. *Dead Bones Live: An Exposition of the Prophecy of Ezekiel*.

_____. *Jude's Apostates*. Eastbourne, Sussex, England: Upperton Press, 1975.

_____. *Paul's Letters to the Thessalonians*. Neptune, NJ: Loizeaux, 1991.

Tenney, Merrill C., Editor. *The Zondervan Pictorial Encyclopedia of the Bible*. Grand Rapids: Zondervan Publishing House, 1979.

Thomas, Robert L. *Understanding Spiritual Gifts*. Grand Rapids: Kregel Publications, 1999.

Thomas, Robert L. and Stanley N. Gundry. *A Harmony of the Gospels*. San Francisco, CA: Harper San Francisco, 1988.

Thomas W. H. Griffith. *Genesis: A Devotional Commentary*. Grand Rapids: Kregel Publications, 1988.

_____. *Studies in Colossians and Philemon*. Grand Rapids: Kregel Publications, 1986.

Toussaint, Stanley D. *Behold the King: A Study in Matthew*. Portland, OR: Multnomah, 1980.

Unger, Merril F. *Unger's Commentary of the Old Testament*. Chicago: Moody Press, 1981.

Vine, W. E. Merril F. Unger, and William White, Jr., *Vine's Expository Dictionary of Old and New Testaments Words*. Nashville TN.: Thomas Nelson Publishers, 1992.

Walvoord, John F. *Matthew: Thy Kingdom Come*. Grand Rapids: Kregel Publications, 1999.

_____. *The Revelation of Jesus Christ*. Chicago: Moody Press, 1966.

Wenham, Gordon J. *Numbers: An Introduction and Commentary.* Tyndale Old Testament Commentaries. Downers Grove, IL: InterVarsity Press, 1981.

Wiersbe, Warren W. *The Bible Exposition Commentary.* Wheaton, IL: Victor Books, 1989.

Wilcock, Michael. *The Message of Chronicles.* Downers Grove, IL: InterVarsity Press, 1987.

Wolf, Herbert. *Haggai and Malachi.* Chicago: Moody Press, 1979.

Wood, Leon J. *The Prophets of Israel.* Grand Rapids: Baker Book House/ Revell, 1981.

Wuest, Kenneth S. *Philippians in the Greek New Testament.* Grand Rapids: Wm. B. Eerdmans Pub. Co., 1948.

Young, Edward J. *My Servants the Prophets.* Grand Rapids: Wm. B. Eerdmans Pub. Co., 1952.

Zuck, Roy B. *Job.* Chicago: Moody Press, 1979.

BIBLE VERSIONS:

The Holy Bible, New International Version. Grand Rapids: Zondervan Corp. Copyright 1984, International Bible Society.

The Holy Bible, New King James Version. Nashville: Thomas Nelson, Inc. 1992.

The New American Standard Bible. LaHabra, CA: The Lockman Foundation, 1977.

Ryrie Study Bible for the NASB, NKJV, NIV.

ACQUISITION CHECKLIST

— ❦ —

	Own	Priority 1	Priority 2
Bible Atlases			
The Macmillan Bible Atlas – AHARONI & AUI-YONAH	❏	❏	❏
The Moody Altas of Bible Lands – BEITZEL	❏	❏	❏
Zondervan NIV Atlas of the Bible – RASMUSSEN	❏	❏	❏
Bible Dictionaries			
The New Unger's Bible Dictionary – HARRISON, VOS, & BARBER	❏	❏	❏
The Zondervan Pictorial Encyclopedia of the Bible – TENNEY	❏	❏	❏
Bibles, Versions, and Concordances			
The New American Standard Bible	❏	❏	❏
New American Standard Exhaustive Concordance of the Bible	❏	❏	❏
The New International Version	❏	❏	❏
The New International Version Complete Concordance – GOODRICH & KOHLENBERGER	❏	❏	❏

	Own	Priority 1	Priority 2
The New King James Version	☐	☐	☐
The New King James Version Exhaustive Concordance	☐	☐	☐
Ryrie Study Bible	☑	☐	☐

Interlinear Testaments

	Own	Priority 1	Priority 2
The Interlinear Hebrew/Greek English Bible – GREEN	☐	☐	☐
The New American Standard Bible Interlinear Greek-English New Testament	☐	☐	☐

Word Studies

	Own	Priority 1	Priority 2
Vine's Expository Dictionary of Old and New Testaments Words – VINE	☑	☐	☐

Other Essential Reference Works

	Own	Priority 1	Priority 2
The Bible Explorer's Guide – PHILLIPS	☐	☐	☐
A General Introduction to the Bible – GEISLER	☐	☐	☐
Living By the Book – HENDRICKS	☑	☐	☐
The Minister's Library – BARBER	☐	☐	☐

Bible Commentaries

	Own	Priority 1	Priority 2
Explore the Book – BAXTER	☐	☐	☐
Gaebelien's Concise Commentary on the Whole Bible – GAEBELIEN	☐	☐	☐
The Ironside Commentary Series – IRONSIDE	☐	☐	☐
The Unfolding Drama of Redemption – SCROGGIE	☐	☐	☐

	Own	Priority 1	Priority 2
Commentaries on the OT			
Unger's Commentary of the Old Testament – UNGER	❑	❑	❑
Commentaries on the NT			
The Bible Exposition Commentary – WIERSBE	❑	❑	❑
Commentary on the New Testament – ERDMAN	❑	❑	❑
Daily Study Bible – BARCLAY	❑	❑	❑
Bible Doctrine			
Evangelical Theology: A Survey and Review – LIGHTNER	❑	❑	❑
Moody Handbook of Theology – ENNS	❑	❑	❑
Church History			
Christianity Through the Centuries – CAIRNS	❑	❑	❑
The Pentateuch			
Handbook on the Pentateuch – HAMILTON	❑	❑	❑
The Pentateuch in Its Cultural Environment – LIVINGSTONE	❑	❑	❑
Genesis			
Exploring Genesis – PHILLIPS	❑	❑	❑
Genesis: A Devotional Commentary – THOMAS	❑	❑	❑
Paradise to Prison: Studies in Genesis – DAVIS	❑	❑	❑

Exodus

	Own	Priority 1	Priority 2
Commentary on Exodus – BUSH	❑	❑	❑
Exodus: An Introduction and Commentary – COLE	❑	❑	❑

Leviticus

God's Prophetic Calendar – STRAUSS	❑	❑	❑
Leviticus, An Introduction and Commentary – HARRISON	❑	❑	❑
Notes on Leviticus – BUSH	❑	❑	❑

Numbers

The Book of Numbers – ERDMAN	❑	❑	❑
Numbers: An Introduction and Commentary – WENHAM	❑	❑	❑

Deuteronomy

The Book of Deuteronomy – ERDMAN	❑	❑	❑
Deuteronomy: The Gospel of Love – SCHULTZ	❑	❑	❑

THE HISTORICAL BOOKS:
Joshua

The Book of Joshua – BLAIKIE	❑	❑	❑
Joshua – ENNS	❑	❑	❑

Judges

Judges: A Narrative of God's Power – BARBER	❑	❑	❑

	Own	Priority 1	Priority 2
Notes of Judges – BUSH	❏	❏	❏

Ruth

Judges and Ruth – CUNDALL & MORRIS	❏	❏	❏
Ruth: A Story of God's Grace – BARBER	❏	❏	❏

The Books of Samuel

1 and 2 Samuel – BALDWIN	❏	❏	❏
The Books of Samuel – BARBER	❏	❏	❏
The First Book of Samuel – BLAIKIE	❏	❏	❏
The Second Book of Samuel – BLAIKIE	❏	❏	❏

The Books of Kings

The Kings of Judah and Israel – KNAPP	❏	❏	❏
Studies in the Books of Kings – KIRK & RAWLINSON	❏	❏	❏

The Books of Chronicles

First and Second Chronicles – SAILHAMER	❏	❏	❏
The Message of Chronicles – WILCOCK	❏	❏	❏

Ezra, Nehemiah, Esther

The Book of Esther – RALEIGH	❏	❏	❏
Ezra and Nehemiah – ADENEY	❏	❏	❏
Nehemiah and the Dynamics of Effective Leadership – BARBER	❏	❏	❏

	Own	Priority 1	Priority 2
Notes on Ezra, Nehemiah, and Esther – IRONSIDE	❏	❏	❏

THE POETICAL BOOKS:
Job

Job – ANDERSON	❏	❏	❏
Job – ZUCK	❏	❏	❏

Psalms

Commentary on the Psalms – PEROWNE	❏	❏	❏
Exploring the Psalms – PHILLIPS	❏	❏	❏

Proverbs

Commentary on Proverbs – LAWSON	❏	❏	❏
Proverbs – IRONSIDE	❏	❏	❏
Studies in Proverbs – ARNOT	❏	❏	❏

Ecclesiastes

A Time to Mourn, a Time to Dance: Ecclesiastes and the Way of the World – KIDNER	❏	❏	❏
Ecclesiastes: Total Life – KAISER	❏	❏	❏
Living on the Ragged Edge – SWINDOLL	❏	❏	❏

Song of Solomon

A Song for Lovers – GLICKMAN	❏	❏	❏
The Song of Solomon – CARR	❏	❏	❏
The Song of Solomon – IRONSIDE	❏	❏	❏

	Own	Priority 1	Priority 2
The Prophetic Books:			
The Prophets of Israel – WOOD	❏	❏	❏
My Servants the Prophets – YOUNG	❏	❏	❏
Isaiah			
An Exposition of the Book of Isaiah – KELLY	❏	❏	❏
Isaiah, Translated and Explained – ALEXANDER	❏	❏	❏
Jeremiah and Lamentations			
A Biblical Approach to Personal Suffering – KAISER	❏	❏	❏
Jeremiah, A Commentary – FEINBERG	❏	❏	❏
Jeremiah and Lamentations – HARRISON	❏	❏	❏
Jeremiah and Lamentations: An Exposition – ERDMAN	❏	❏	❏
Ezekiel			
Dead Bones Live: An Exposition of the Prophecy of Ezekiel – TATFORD	❏	❏	❏
Ezekiel – ALEXANDER	❏	❏	❏
Ezekiel – ENNS	❏	❏	❏
Daniel			
Daniel and His Prophecy – TATFORD	❏	❏	❏
Daniel and the Latter Days – CULVER	❏	❏	❏

	Own	Priority 1	Priority 2
Exploring the Book of Daniel – PHILLIPS & VINES	❏	❏	❏

The Minor Prophets

	Own	Priority 1	Priority 2
The Minor Prophets – BOICE	❏	❏	❏
The Minor Prophets – IRONSIDE	❏	❏	❏

Hosea

	Own	Priority 1	Priority 2
The Message of Hosea – KIDNER	❏	❏	❏

Joel

	Own	Priority 1	Priority 2
Joel – ALLEN	❏	❏	❏

Amos

	Own	Priority 1	Priority 2
The Message of Amos – MOTYER	❏	❏	❏

Obadiah

	Own	Priority 1	Priority 2
Four Minor Prophets: Obadiah, Jonah, Habakkuk, and Haggai – GAEBELIEN	❏	❏	❏

Jonah

	Own	Priority 1	Priority 2
Jonah: An Exposition – KENDALL	❏	❏	❏
Jonah: His Life and Time – KIRK	❏	❏	❏
Jonah: Meeting the God of the Second Chance – HAWKINS	❏	❏	❏
The Prophet Jonah – BURN	❏	❏	❏

Micah

	Own	Priority 1	Priority 2
Micah – RIGGS	❏	❏	❏

	Own	Priority 1	Priority 2

Nahum

Jonah and Nahum – KOHLENBERGER   ❏   ❏   ❏

Habakkuk

Habakkuk and Zephaniah – BARBER   ❏   ❏   ❏

Zephaniah

A Shelter in the Fury – ALLEN   ❏   ❏   ❏

Haggai

Haggai and Malachi – WOLF   ❏   ❏   ❏

Zechariah

God Remembers: A Study of Zechariah   ❏   ❏   ❏
   – FEINBERG

Malachi

Malachi: God's Unchanging Love – KAISER   ❏   ❏   ❏

Where Are You, God? – OSWALT   ❏   ❏   ❏

Life of Christ

The Crisis of the Christ – MORGAN   ❏   ❏   ❏

The Great Physician – MORGAN   ❏   ❏   ❏

The Life of Christ – CULVER   ❏   ❏   ❏

The Words and Works of Jesus Christ – PENTECOST   ❏   ❏   ❏

The Gospels

A Harmony of the Gospels – THOMAS & GUNDRY   ❏   ❏   ❏

	Own	Priority 1	Priority 2
Guide to the Gospels – SCROGGIE	❏	❏	❏

Matthew

Behold the King – TOUSSAINT	❏	❏	❏
Matthew: Thy Kingdom Come – WALVOORD	❏	❏	❏

Mark

The Gospel of Mark: An Introduction and Commentary – COLE	❏	❏	❏
Mark: A Portrait of the Servant – HIEBERT	❏	❏	❏
The Ruler Who Serves – STEDMAN	❏	❏	❏
The Servant Who Rules – STEDMAN	❏	❏	❏

Luke

Gospel of Luke – GODET	❏	❏	❏
The Gospel According to St. Luke – MORRIS	❏	❏	❏

John

Exploring the Gospels: John – PHILLIPS	❏	❏	❏
The Gospel of John – BOICE	❏	❏	❏
Light in the Darkness – KENT	❏	❏	❏

Acts

The Acts of the Apostles – BRUCE	❏	❏	❏
The Acts of the Apostles – MORGAN	❏	❏	❏
Acts of the Apostles – RYRIE	❏	❏	❏

	Own	Priority 1	Priority 2
The Spirit, the Church, and the World – STOTT	❑	❑	❑

The Apostle Paul

Personalities Around Paul – HIEBERT	❑	❑	❑
Paul the Traveller – BRADFORD	❑	❑	❑

Romans

Commentary on Romans – GODET	❑	❑	❑
The Letter of Paul to the Romans – BRUCE	❑	❑	❑
Romans: Righteousness from Heaven – HUGHES	❑	❑	❑

The Corinthian Epistles

Called To Be Saints – GROMACKI	❑	❑	❑
Expository Studies in 2 Corinthians – STEDMAN	❑	❑	❑
First Corinthians – HUGHES	❑	❑	❑
Paul's Second Epistle to the Corinthians – HUGHES	❑	❑	❑
Stand Firm in the Faith – GROMACKI	❑	❑	❑
Understanding Spiritual Gifts – THOMAS	❑	❑	❑

Galatians

Flesh and Spirit – BARCLAY	❑	❑	❑
The Freedom of God's Sons: Studies in Galatians – KENT	❑	❑	❑
Letter of Paul to the Galatians – COLE	❑	❑	❑

	Own	Priority 1	Priority 2
The Message of Galatians – STOTT	❏	❏	❏

Ephesians

Ephesians – MACARTHUR	❏	❏	❏
Ephesians: The Mystery of the Body of Christ – HUGHES	❏	❏	❏
Exploring Ephesians – PHILLIPS	❏	❏	❏
God's New Society: The Message of Ephesians – STOTT	❏	❏	❏
Spiritual Warfare – STEDMAN	❏	❏	❏

Philippians

Devotional Studies in Philippians – STRAUSS	❏	❏	❏
The Joy of Living – PENTECOST	❏	❏	❏
Philippians in the Greek New Testament – WUEST	❏	❏	❏

Colossians

Colossians and Philemon: The Supremacy of Christ – HUGHES	❏	❏	❏
Studies in Colossians and Philemon – THOMAS	❏	❏	❏

The Thessalonian Epistles

The Epistles to the Thessalonians – RYRIE	❏	❏	❏
Paul's Letters to the Thessalonians – TATFORD	❏	❏	❏

	Own	Priority 1	Priority 2
The Thessalonian Epistles – HIEBERT	❏	❏	❏

The Pastoral Epistles

First Timothy – HIEBERT	❏	❏	❏
Guard the Gospel – STOTT	❏	❏	❏
The Pastoral Epistles – GUTHRIE	❏	❏	❏
The Pastoral Epistles – KENT	❏	❏	❏
Second Timothy – HIEBERT	❏	❏	❏
Titus and Philemon – HIEBERT	❏	❏	❏

Philemon

The Epistle to Phlemon – COX & DRYSDALE	❏	❏	❏
Studies in Philemon – SCROGGIE	❏	❏	❏

Hebrews

A Commentary on the Epistle to the Hebrews – HUGHES	❏	❏	❏
The Epistle to the Hebrews – BRUCE	❏	❏	❏
The Letter to the Hebrews – GUTHRIE	❏	❏	❏

James

The Epistle of James: Tests of a Living Faith – HIEBERT	❏	❏	❏
James Your Brother – STRAUSS	❏	❏	❏

	Own	Priority 1	Priority 2

The Epistles of Peter

A Practical Commentary Upon the First Epistle of Peter – LEIGHTON   ❑ ❑ ❑

The First Epistle General of Peter – STIBBS   ❑ ❑ ❑

First Peter – HIEBERT   ❑ ❑ ❑

The Second Epistle General of Peter and The General Epistle of Jude – GREEN   ❑ ❑ ❑

Second Peter and Jude – HIEBERT   ❑ ❑ ❑

The Johannine Epistles

The Epistles of John – HIEBERT   ❑ ❑ ❑

The Epistles of John – STRAUSS   ❑ ❑ ❑

The Epistles of John – STOTT   ❑ ❑ ❑

The Epistle of Jude

The Acts of the Apostates – CODER   ❑ ❑ ❑

Beware of Pretenders – MACARTHUR   ❑ ❑ ❑

Jude's Apostates – TATFORD   ❑ ❑ ❑

Revelation

The Book of Revelation – MORRIS   ❑ ❑ ❑

Letters to the Seven Churches – BARCLAY   ❑ ❑ ❑

The Revelation of Jesus Christ – WALVOORD   ❑ ❑ ❑

The Revelation of John – BARCLAY   ❑ ❑ ❑

ADDITIONAL
INFORMATION

— ❧ —

The Minister's Library
Cyril J. Barber

For years Christian professionals have let their book purchasing be guided by *The Minister's Library*, the most comprehensive guide to Christian literature available. Loizeaux has now updated this invaluable resource and published it in electronoic format. The searchable database includes information about thousands of books from the great classics of years past to recently published titles and is updated annually.

CD-ROM for Windows • ISBN: 1-57822-050-5

Book Purchases

The titles listed in Best Books may be purchased from your local Christian retailer. Many of them can also be purchased directly from Loizeaux by visiting our web site.

LOIZEAUX
PO Box 277
Neptune, NJ 07754

1-800-526-2796

www.loizeaux.org